THE 29% SOLUTION

52 Weekly Networking Success Strategies

IVAN R. MISNER, PhD
and Michelle R. Donovan

GREENLEAF
BOOK GROUP PRESS

Published by Greenleaf Book Group Press
4425 S. Mo Pac Expy., Suite 600
Austin, TX 78735

Distributed by Greenleaf Book Group LLC

For ordering information or special discounts for bulk purchases, please contact Greenleaf Book Group LLC at 4425 S. Mo Pac Expy., Suite 600, Austin, TX 78735, (512) 891-6100.

Design and composition by Greenleaf Book Group LLC
Cover design by Greenleaf Book Group LLC

Publisher's Cataloging-In-Publication Data
(Prepared by The Donohue Group, Inc.)

Misner, Ivan R., 1956-
    The 29% solution : 52 weekly networking success strategies / Ivan R. Misner, with Michelle R. Donovan. -- 1st ed.

    p. ; cm.

    Includes bibliographical references and index.
    ISBN: 978-1-929774-54-8

1. Business networks. 2. Success in business. 3. Social networks. 4. Interpersonal relations. I. Donovan, Michelle R. (Michelle Rose) II. Title. III. Title: Twenty-nine per cent solution

HD69.S8 M576 2008
650.1/3   2008923310

Printed in the United States of America on acid-free paper

13 12 11 10 09 08   10 9 8 7 6 5 4 3 2

First Edition

CONTENTS

PREFACE

(One You Should Really Read!)

WHAT DO SANTA CLAUS, THE EASTER BUNNY, and "six degrees of separation" have in common? Answer: People all around the world believe in them.

Now, we're not going to do an exposé on Kris Kringle or the egg-laying rabbit. We don't want to stir up trouble. What we do want is to take issue with the six-degrees thing.

You've heard that there are "six degrees of separation" between you and anybody else on earth that you would like to meet. Right?

Amazing, isn't it?

Ain't true.

Sorry, we hate to burst your bubble on such a lovely idea, but it's one of those urban myths that have grown from a small kernel of truth.

The legend originally stems from several "small world" experiments conducted by Stanley Milgram in the '60s and '70s. These experiments involved sending letters from a group of people in one part of the country to a specific person (whom they did not know) in another part of the country. The participants were told to get the material to someone who might know someone who would know the individual to whom the material was to be delivered. This process formed a chain of connections linking the people together.

It was, in fact, found that the letters that eventually arrived in the right person's hands took, on average, between five and six connections, or degrees. This part is true; however, if you look closer, you will discover the problems that exist within the blanket statement that "we are all connected by six degrees."

First off, though the average number of links for people who got the material to the final contact was five or six connections, the majority of the connections made ranged from two to ten. This means that roughly half took more than six and roughly half less than six. Well, you say, that's the average, and we would agree that there's nothing wrong with addressing this concept by the average, but there's one small problem: the overwhelming majority of people in all of the "small world" studies never got the material to the intended recipient at all!

In Milgram's most successful study, "217 chains were started and 64 were completed—a success rate of only 29%."[1] That's right—a success rate of less than one-third of the participants! This means that 29 percent of the people in Milgram's most successful study were separated on average by six degrees from the final contact person. However, it also means that 71 percent were not connected at all!

But wait, we're afraid it gets worse. This was Milgram's most successful study. In another of his studies, only 5 percent of the participants completed the chain, which means that 95 percent of the people in the study never made the link to the person with whom they were to connect at all—ever!

Don't shoot the messenger, but we must tell you that we are not "all" connected with everyone in the world by six degrees of separation. We're just not . . . not all of us. But why would the authors of a book on networking be telling readers about the Achilles' heel of this iconic concept upon which a lot of networking pros hang their hats? There are two reasons.

First of all, we believe this myth creates complacency. The thought that everyone is absolutely connected to everyone else on the planet by six degrees gives some people a false expectation, lulling them into the impression that the connection is bound to happen sooner or later, no matter what they do. Second, and most importantly, the studies' findings indicate clearly that some people are better connected than others. We believe that's important, because it means that "connecting" is a skill that can be acquired. With reading, training, and coaching, people can develop their networking skills, increase their connections, and become part of the roughly 29 percent of people who are, in fact, separated from the rest of the world by just six degrees.

> **With reading, training, and coaching, people can develop their networking skills, increase their connections, and become part of the roughly 29 percent of people who are, in fact, separated from the rest of the world by just six degrees.**

Milgram's work was revolutionary, to be sure. It opened up a whole new world of discussion and understanding. It has also, however, been romanticized. The mythical version of his findings does no good for anyone. It gives people a false sense of security and/or an erroneous worldview from a networking standpoint.

We do believe that we live in a "small world" that is becoming smaller and smaller; we also believe it is possible to be connected to anyone in the world by only six degrees. We just don't believe that we are *all* connected by six degrees, and Milgram's own findings support that.

The good news in all of this is that it is possible to be part of the 29 percent through education, practice, and training. We can be connected to anyone through the power and potential of networking. In fact, by understanding that, we can set ourselves aside from our competition by knowing that being able to make successful connections is not an entitlement. Instead, it is a skill that only some actually develop.

We believe that you would like to be a part of that 29 percent. Why? Because you want to improve your networking skills, that's why! It's a no-brainer. The smaller the number of phone calls, letters, e-mails, lunches, and road trips between you and someone's ideal client somewhere in the world, the more value you bring to your networking partners, and the stronger and more prosperous your business networking becomes.

That's one reason you need to read this book. Here's another:

A survey of more than 2,200 businesspeople at BNI.com revealed that 87 percent had never had a college course that even mentioned networking. We're not talking about an entire course on the subject (they are outnumbered by unicorns); we mean any course that even brushed on the topic. Yet, in another survey of more than 3,800 businesspeople worldwide, 73 percent said they got most of their business through networking!

Networking, which can help you build word-of-mouth marketing, is one of the most important ways for entrepreneurs to grow their businesses. More than eight out of ten businesspeople belong to some type of networking group (according to an online survey at BNI.com of over 5,000 people), yet virtually no colleges or universities offer a course on the subject.

Can this possibly be true? Six degrees of separation shot full of holes, and colleges don't teach networking? It's almost too much to handle. We give people bachelor's degrees in marketing, business, and even entrepreneurship, but we teach them next to nothing about the one subject that virtually every entrepreneur knows to be critical to his business.

Why don't business schools teach networking/word-of-mouth marketing? We think it's because most such schools are staffed by full-time professors who've never owned a business in their lives.

Almost everything they've learned about running a business comes from books and consulting. Obviously these professors, who are not practitioners, don't understand the importance of networking for entrepreneurs. Can you imagine a law course taught by someone who's not an attorney, or an accounting course taught by anyone without direct accounting experience? We humbly suggest that if you haven't actually owned a business, you might have a handicap in teaching a course on entrepreneurship.

Business schools worldwide need to wake up and start teaching this curriculum. Schools with vision and foresight and the ability to act swiftly (sort of the way business professors claim that businesses should act) will be positioning themselves as leaders in education by understanding and responding to the needs of today's entrepreneurs. Business schools are, however, as bureaucratic as any large institution, so it's unlikely to happen quickly. That's too bad. Why?

Word-of-mouth marketing works. Social capital is vital. And networking is the mechanism to develop both. As more universities and colleges open their doors to professors who want to include this strategy in their marketing curriculum, we'll see a major shift in the business education landscape. We'll see emerging entrepreneurs who are equipped with another tactic for success. We'll see networking utilized to its fullest capacity, and we'll see business schools actually teaching a subject that the business practitioner says is important.

What a thought. Oh well, it's good to have goals.

As of this writing, we know of two schools that offer regular, core-curriculum, college-level courses on networking and social capital. The first is the University of Michigan. Its class is taught by Wayne Baker, co-owner of Humax Corporation in Ann Arbor. The second is Davis College in Ohio, and their class is taught by a friend of ours, Debby Peters. Debby uses the networking curriculum called the Certified Networker Program (www.certifiednetworker.com), developed by the Referral Institute (www.ReferralInstitute.com).

Of the thousands of colleges and universities all around the world, only these two have a core-curriculum course on the subject of networking. Is it any wonder that most businesspeople are so hungry to learn how to improve this part of their business? Congratulations go to these leaders in the field for teaching something that every college should be teaching.

So, with (almost) no college courses available and few on the horizon, what are your options for getting good networking training? It's continuing education or nothing. There are a few good resources available for training outside of college, and there are a lot of good books. For more on these, we refer you to the final chapter of this book, "Week 52 Strategy: Commit to Lifelong Learning," which discusses how you can become your own faculty advisor and design a continuing education curriculum for the art and science of business networking.

But first, we want to congratulate you on choosing this book to start with—because *The 29% Solution* is, we believe, a great way to bring yourself up to networking speed in a systematic, practical, observable way. And you don't have to swallow it in one big gulp. It's designed to lead you through a series of exercises, one per week, over a year. This allows you to spend an entire week incorporating each networking activity into your business routine. You don't have to do the exercises in any particular order. You can skip ahead, jump back, go directly to exercises that fit your current week's activities, or fill a gap in your skill set. It's about as user-friendly a book as has been written for a busy professional. And a built-in self-assessment (see introduction) will allow you to pat yourself on the back (or rake yourself over the coals) in the privacy of your own office (hold my calls, please).

Many of you may feel that you are at the top of your game in some areas. If that's the case, feel free to concentrate only on the strategies that you judge to be most valuable to you. But it's still a good idea to at least read and think about the weekly strategies where you're already in pretty good shape, and even run through those exercises. It never hurts to check your assumptions, and it's good exercise for the networking muscle.

By the way, for the 71 percent of people who are not connected but still believe in the six-degrees-of-separation concept—keep the faith. You'll always have Santa Claus.

INTRODUCTION

IT'S NOT "NET-SIT" OR "NET-EAT"—IT'S "NETWORK." Successful networking is about learning how to "work" the networking process—not just letting it happen.

In many ways, success at networking is the perfect example of the uncommon application of common knowledge.[1] Most people understand that networking is important to their success—they just lack a step-by-step process to get the results they want. Almost no one really incorporates a comprehensive methodology that will build a business through networking. Thus, the need to network is "common knowledge," and the development of the methodology required to be successful at it is the "uncommon application."

By reading this book, you will experience the true essence and meaning of networking. *The 29% Solution* primarily addresses two conflicting questions that a business owner or salesperson faces every day: How can I tend to my existing clients while at the same time be out networking for new business? and, Should I place higher value on my current clients or on new clients?

The word *networking* has become so overused that some business professionals can no longer define it. Many people think that networking is attending social or business after-hour events, shaking a few hands, collecting a few cards, and, of course, giving away a few cards of their own. Sadly, they actually believe that's all there is to networking. To be fair, we could say they're engaging in social networking. That's never to be confused, however, with business networking. You'll see why as you turn these pages.

We've found that businesspeople tend to fall into one of two groups when it comes to their views of networking. For many, the current mind-set is that networking is a passive business strategy, not a proactive marketing tool. This attitude results in a scattered, often ineffective networking approach that consequently wastes the business owner's time and money. Not surprisingly, when people feel they've been wasting their time and money on something, they're understandably not going to continue that activity.

> **For many, the current mind-set is that networking is a passive business strategy, not a proactive marketing tool.**

On the other hand, some proprietors do consider networking a proactive marketing tool for their business. How can you tell? They make it a significant part of their marketing and business plans. They have networking goals. They may even have a budget line item for networking. Most importantly, they practice it and live it every day.

Which view do you take? If you share the first mind-set—the passive one—you're hoping that just showing up at meetings is enough. And therein lies the problem. But before you finish reading *The 29% Solution*, we're betting you will become—if you're not already—a staunch member of the second group, the proactives.

Whatever your own current state of mind, by purchasing this book, you've already set yourself apart from some other business owners. Your willingness to read *The 29% Solution* demonstrates your ambition to realize the full potential of networking for your business.

The 29% Solution is the first book designed to integrate networking into the way you do business on a weekly basis. This approach truly brings networking into your business as a proactive marketing tool. You will find in these pages fifty-two quick, straightforward networking strategies. Each strategy offers a specific focus for each week over a one-year period. We invite you to incorporate these proven strategies into your weekly planner, PDA, and Outlook calendar.

Incorporate these proven strategies into your weekly planner!

Building these strategies into your life helps you maintain your focus on networking while you work to identify new revenue streams for your business. Before you know it, you'll be driven by the intention to get new business, and you'll have the networking tools to satisfy that drive, because—let's face it—if you have no new business, soon you will have no business at all.

What Is Business Networking?

Networking is the process of developing contacts and relationships to increase your business, enhance your knowledge, expand your sphere of influence, or serve the community. In its most basic form, "business networking" is leveraging your business and personal connections to bring you a regular supply of new business. The concept sounds awfully simple, doesn't it? Don't let that fool you, though. Because it involves relationship building, it can be a deceptively complex process.

Think about it. How many people do you know? How many of these people truly understand what you do? How many of these folks have directed prospects to you as referrals? And how many of those referrals have actually turned into business?

Business networking is much more than showing up at networking functions, shaking a lot of hands, and collecting a bunch of cards. Here's an example of what we mean.

Imagine two people entering an event, sizing it up, and drawing an imaginary line down the middle. They separate, each taking half the room. At the end of the event, they meet again to see who's collected the most business cards.

Have you met these people? Sure you have. We all have. What did they accomplish? They collected a lot of cards that will end up on a shelf, in a drawer, in the trash, or—worse yet—scanned into a computer so they can spam everyone they just met. Why? What does a business card represent? At this point, in reality, it's a piece of paper, with ink and images on it. No relationship has been formed. This networking strategy, by itself, isn't an effective use of time, money, or energy.

Some people get frustrated with networking because they seem to be making as much progress as a rear-wheel-drive truck on an icy hill: one foot forward, ten feet back—getting nowhere fast. Networking for business growth must be strategic and focused. Not everyone you meet can help move your business forward— but everything you do can be driven by the intention to grow your business. You have total control over who you meet, where you meet them, and how you develop and leverage relationships for mutual benefit. You have total control over whether you enter into the unique 29% of the population who are separated by six degrees, whether you stay there, or whether you never get there at all.

Networking your business means you have to be proactive. That's why we say, "It's not net-SIT or net-EAT—it's net-WORK!"

The fifty-two weekly strategies outlined in this book will help you focus your efforts so that you'll begin to reap the benefits of effective business networking. We recommend that you begin with the first section: Create Your Future. It's designed to be the starting point and direct you toward profitable networking. After this first section, however, you need not proceed in order. If you see a strategy farther ahead that appears to be particularly timely and helpful for your business, jump ahead in the book and do it. The point is to do something specific each week that is focused on networking for business growth. Remember: this is your plan, and you lead the activity.

Why Be GOOD When GREAT Is an Option?

In his book *Good to Great*, Jim Collins shares many examples of how great companies are different from good companies. In many situations, the differences are in the little things that are done exceptionally well. So it is with networking your business: great networkers in the 29% produce exceptional results. Once you decide to be great, good is no longer an option.

Great networkers move their businesses forward, but they don't do it alone. Great networkers have a plan, work to expand their network, go the extra mile, know how to get the most value for their time, communicate their messages effectively, become the experts, capture their best stories, and do what others don't do. People are drawn to them. New clients go to them because they hear about them from so many people. Great networkers don't need to do much selling, because many people come to them, ready to buy.

> **Great networkers don't need to do much selling,**
> **because many people come to them, ready to buy.**

Imagine that! People coming to you, ready to buy! Are you smiling? You should be. Becoming a great, effective networker is within your reach. Your income is directly related to your ability to network your business for growth. Are you ready to get started? Are you committed to actively growing your business by word of mouth? Have you decided that now is the time for you to advance from good to great?

If you're ready, then let's begin by discovering how well you are networking your business right now. What are you doing well, and what are you doing not so well? You have to understand this in order to know where you're going.

We know this can be difficult. Looking at yourself in a mirror—and asking others to look at you too—can feel pretty uncomfortable. Hey, we've been there. Now we're better and wiser for the experience. You will be too.

We've made the process a little easier by providing a structured self-assessment tool. In the brief exercise that follows, identify your strengths and weaknesses. Be honest. Be brutally honest. Ask others for their perception of you as well.

Every point referenced in the assessment will be addressed in this book. Thus, completing this self-assessment will help you get the most out of *The 29% Solution*. It will help you focus on specific goals and accountabilities—and, without a doubt, it will keep you focused on the true meaning of business networking.

THE 29% SOLUTION SELF-ANALYSIS

For each answer, respond with 1 to 5 (1 = not at all; 5 = all the time).

____ 1. I have written long-term networking goals.

____ 2. I block out time in my weekly schedule for regular networking activities.

____ 3. I can profile my preferred client as well as a TV profiler.

____ 4. I have a strong team of referral partners.

____ 5. I live by the "Givers Gain" philosophy (I give business to others before I expect them to give business to me).

____ 6. I have an organized contact management system that I use effectively.

____ 7. I know the top ten traits of a master networker.

____ 8. I have a very diverse personal network (people from differing professions, ethnicity, age, education, gender, etc.).

____ 9. I know who can get me to my target market.

____ 10. I keep in contact with people from organizations I used to belong to.

____ 11. I make sure that my brother/sister/parent/family member can accurately explain what I do for a living.

____ 12. I attend at least two networking functions or activities per week.

____ 13. I belong to a Web-based networking group.

____ 14. I am someone whom people seek out when they need help.

____ 15. I bring personal value to my relationships.

____ 16. I typically am the one who puts the wheels in motion in a networking relationship.

____ 17. I have a networking accountability partner.

____ 18. I am an active volunteer for something meaningful to my life.

____ 19. I send thank-you cards regularly.

____ 20. I consistently follow up on referrals within twenty-four hours.

____ 21. I have found myself networking in the grocery store or elevator.

____ 22. I capitalize on my hobbies to meet people.

____ 23. I make the focus of my lunchtime meetings how I can help the other person.

____ 24. I am good at making a connection when I meet someone new.

____ 25. I am an active member of a referral networking group.

____ 26. I am an active member of a chamber of commerce.

___ 27. I sponsor at least one event per year for a referral partner.

___ 28. I host an event for the people in my network several times a year.

___ 29. I am skilled at asking the right questions of a networking contact.

___ 30. I have created my message to be about the customer benefits of my product or service rather than its features.

___ 31. I can consistently describe my target market without saying "anybody."

___ 32. I make sure that people hear the passion in my voice when I talk about my business.

___ 33. I make a good first impression with my business card.

___ 34. I provide information that is valuable to my audience whenever I give a presentation.

___ 35. I send a newsletter to my business's clients.

___ 36. I regularly put out press releases for my business.

___ 37. I have written articles for publication.

___ 38. I make getting client testimonials a part of my sales process.

___ 39. I have provided my referral partners with success stories about my business.

___ 40. I have prepared a written introduction for each time I am presented to a group.

___ 41. I am comfortable sharing my accomplishments.

___ 42. I make a practice of asking for feedback from clients.

___ 43. I start new networking relationships by acting like a host at networking events.

___ 44. I have asked my vendors for referrals.

___ 45. I provide support to my target market beyond my services.

___ 46. I ask for referrals every day.

___ 47. I look for referrals for others daily.

___ 48. I am comfortable speaking in public.

___ 49. I surround myself with others who can help my clients.

___ 50. I mentor others in the art, science, and philosophy of networking.

___ 51. I have an advisory board for my business.

___ 52. I enjoy learning more about how to network effectively.

Total Score: _____

Scoring

260   Master Networker

You should be writing the next book! There is no doubt that your networking skills are remarkable. Most likely, you already are in the 29% of the population who truly are separated by six degrees. Your challenge now is to stay there! This book will focus your efforts and remind you of things that may have been lost along the way.

234–259   Outstanding

Way to go! You are in the 90th percentile. Clearly, you know how to network. You are most likely skilled enough to be approaching the 29%. Your thirst for learning will have you devouring this book and learning strategies to further improve the return on your investment of effort in networking and, with commitment, move you into the 29%.

208–233   Very Good

You are in the 80th percentile. You're doing many things right. Your effort can be very effective, and your relationships strong. This book will help you focus your plan and hone your skills to improve your efforts even more, continuing to keep you moving toward that special 29% of the population.

182–207   Good

You're in the 70th percentile. The great thing is—you believe in networking! You clearly see the value in getting into the 29%. However, there's still a fair amount for you to learn. This book will forever change the way you view the process. It will focus your energy and give you the system you so desperately seek in order to gain a high return on your networking investment. You're in for a treat!

156–181   Fair

You are in the 60th percentile. On the bright side, you're probably building some good relationships around you. You most likely have people who care about you and want to help you and your business grow. They can be a resource to help teach you how to move toward the 29%. However, you could be doing some things that will hurt your business with respect to networking. This book will refocus your efforts and help you move further into the networking arena, one strategy at a time.

130–155   Weak

You are in the 50th percentile. Networking is an acquired skill. This book will help you realize the skill base you need in order to network your business. If you're ready to connect more closely with people and learn the skills necessary to be in the 29%, you've bought the right book. The world is waiting to know more about you and your business!

0–129   Help!

You're in the 40th percentile or lower. Quick! Read on!

Understanding Your Results

So what was your score? Before we move into Section One, let's take a few moments to talk about what the results of your self-assessment mean for you.

First off, your score is between you and yourself alone. It's not meant to be shared anywhere outside your own head.

Whatever your score, remember that you're simply taking your networking temperature, so to speak—not engaging in any value judgments about yourself, one way or the other. Indeed, if you take this self-assessment a few months from now, the score will probably be different—assuming you read the rest of this book and practice some of the strategies with ongoing commitment!

SECTION ONE
CREATE YOUR FUTURE

WITH THE RESULTS OF YOUR SELF-ASSESSMENT fresh in your mind, let's start creating your future—right here at the beginning, with Section One. Now that you are more aware of your networking strengths and weaknesses, you can be realistic about the kinds of goals and plans you should make. Remember, you want to tailor the weekly strategies in *The 29% Solution* to fit the "real you"—not the "ideal you"—because you won't reach your ideal over time unless you're clear with yourself about what you need to work on to improve your networking skills.

Just as when building a new house, you need a strong, stable foundation on which to construct your "networking home." We devote the first seven weeks to helping you set goals, develop a plan, and accomplish other essential steps.

Just as when building a new house, you need a strong, stable foundation on which to construct your "networking home."

By way of introduction, let's walk through an overview of the first seven weekly strategies that will get you started.

We recommend that you start with the Week 1 Strategy ("Set Networking Goals"). Networking goals are vital. They keep you focused on the steps needed to network your business every day. Please pay careful attention to this process.

In the Week 2 Strategy ("Block Out Time to Network"), you are challenged to carve out time in your weekly schedule for networking. Reading this book is only one step toward strengthening your business network and getting into the 29%. To meet your goals, you must dedicate time to networking.

The Week 3 Strategy ("Profile Your Preferred Client") asks you to describe your preferred client in very specific and strategic terms. Knowing exactly who you want to attract to your business as a client or customer—and being able to clearly, concisely, and quickly describe that preferred client to everyone from your mother all the way down to the CEO of a Fortune 500 firm—is a vital step for networking success.

The Week 4 Strategy ("Recruit Your Word-of-Mouth Marketing Team") shows you how to begin recruiting the individuals who will serve as your ambassadors. They are critical to your success. Why? Because networking, by definition, is a team sport. You win only when others are winning alongside you.

Our Week 5 Strategy ("Give to Others First") builds on Week 4 and begins to demonstrate the power of the law of reciprocity in networking. This strategy focuses on the benefits of giving to others in your network first, before expecting anything in return. As they say in BNI, the world's largest business networking organization, "Givers gain!" (More on this later.)

The Week 6 Strategy ("Create a Network Relationship Database") directs you to organize the people you know into a network database. An organized network database saves you time and energy in the long run.

Finally, the Week 7 Strategy ("Master the Top Ten Traits") sets a high bar for you to clear: it outlines what a survey of businesspeople deemed the top ten characteristics that define a master net-worker. These same characteristics are what we feel separates those who are in the 29% from those who are not. It gives you some-thing to aim for and a way of assessing where you stand now, rela-tive to that goal.

OK, that's where we're headed for the next seven weeks. Now, let's get going!

☑ WEEK 1

Set Networking Goals

DO YOU HAVE GOALS FOR YOUR BUSINESS? Do you have marketing goals and sales goals? This is a perfect example of the concept we mentioned earlier: the "uncommon application of common knowledge." We all know intellectually that goals are important. The question is, how well do we apply that knowledge?

How about networking goals? If you don't have any, believe it or not, you are in the majority. Obviously you believe in the power of networking or you would not have purchased this book. Why, then, have you not written networking goals for your business?

Networking seems to be one of those things that many people do as a reaction to no or slow business. It often gets forgotten. It is rarely treated as an integral part of how we grow our businesses. Not only is it frequently neglected, but most people are haphazard in their approach to networking, and far from systematic. This approach to networking can keep you from ever getting close to the 29%. This first strategy helps you avoid the pitfalls of treating networking as an afterthought—as something far less than what it can be for your business.

One way to systematize and organize your approach to networking is to set measurable networking goals. As our friend Deanna Tucci Schmitt (owner of BNI Western Pennsylvania) often says, "Without a goal, you have nothing at which to aim."[1] We would add that if you don't have a goal, you can't measure your results. "That which gets written, gets done," as our colleague Tom Fleming in Florida would say.

> **One way to systematize and organize your approach to networking is to set measurable networking goals.**

SMART Goals

Each goal you create should be SMART: Specific, Measurable, Attainable, Relevant, and Timed with a deadline. Let's take a moment to clarify the concept of a SMART goal.

Specific. The goal must be clearly defined with parameters that state who, what, when, where, and how. Specific goals help you stay focused on one thing at a time. For example, stating that you want to become a member of a networking group is fine, but you can define your goal more clearly by saying that you want to become a member of a specific chamber or a particular BNI chapter.

Measurable. The goal must include a way of measuring the results. This typically means that there is a number associated with the goal, such as how many or what percentage—some quantifiable way to measure progress toward the goal. Stating that you want to receive more referrals this year is neither specific nor measurable; it's more useful to say specifically that you want a 30 percent increase in your referral business from a networking group.

Attainable. Each goal that you create must be within reach. It should not be so far-fetched that it's out of your vision. To determine whether a goal is attainable, consider what you accomplished this year. Then consider what you have coming up next year that may either impede or improve your ability to meet a specific goal. Finally, consider everything that needs to be done to accomplish your goal. When all is said and done, do you honestly feel that with hard work, dedication, and focus, you can meet this goal? If so, write it down and commit to achieving it.

Relevant. The goal must have relevance and meaning for you; otherwise, you will not be motivated to accomplish it. What will be the outcome if you meet a particular goal? Will you make more money? Will you have a higher quality of life? Will you be able to save for retirement more comfortably? Will you get a promotion or a raise? Will you save time in the long run? Whatever your personal motivation, ensure that your goals tap into it. Doing so will inspire you every day to keep striving toward the finish line.

Timed. Speaking of a finish line, the goal must have a deadline or completion date assigned to it. Without one, you will lose your focus and your desire to meet your goal in a timely manner. Our human competitive nature draws us to the finish line. We need to aim for a target. For example, stating that you want a 30 percent increase in your referral business from your participation in a networking group is indeed specific and measurable, but how long will it take, and when will you measure it? Stating that you want a 30 percent increase in your annual referral business from the organization by December 31 will be much more effective, because it contains a deadline.

When you put all of these elements together, you might end up with a goal statement that looks like one of these:

- I will become a member of the ABC Chamber by June 30.
- I will achieve a 30 percent increase in my annual referral business from networking in [a certain networking group] by December 31.

We know that setting goals—"SMART" goals—can be difficult. But we've also seen how powerful they can be, as well as the consequences of not giving them their due. Collectively, your two coauthors have written many training curricula. Each one starts with the goal in mind. We've been well trained, for how can we even begin to organize material into a training seminar without first having the end in mind? We typically formulate a set of questions that must be answered before we can move ahead to designing the curriculum.

Steven Covey validates this concept in his *The 7 Habits of Highly Effective People*. One of his strategies is to "begin with the end in mind."[2] The questions below, adapted from his book, will help you focus on what you want to accomplish through networking. Once you begin your own goal-setting process, however, don't limit yourself to these questions.

Week 1 Action

Your task this week is to answer—in writing, not simply in your head—each of the following questions as honestly and as fully as you can. They will provide a structure that will help you create your goal statements. Besides, you have to set your goals before you can design a plan for meeting them. We'll focus on developing that plan in Week 2, so we encourage you to approach this goal-setting process with enthusiasm and diligence. (Remember, you're building that foundation for your networking home!)

Questions for Sample Networking GOALS

1. How much business do you want to get from word-of-mouth referrals, and by when?
   - What do you need to do for this to happen?
   - Who will bring you this business?
   - What kind of business do you expect to get from referrals?
   - Will the referrals focus on a specific product or service?

2. How many networking functions will you attend each month?

   • How will you find out about these functions?

   • What will you accomplish at these functions?

3. How many referrals do you want each week? Each month?

4. How many of the techniques in this book will you begin each month?

5. What five things will you do differently to network your business?

6. With whom do you want to meet this year? (List anything that comes to mind: businesses, professions, names of specific people you'd like to meet.)

7. Of which networking groups would you like to become a member this year?

Additional Exercise

Although we don't want you to get too far ahead of the process, you might choose now to flip through these pages and identify a few strategies that look appropriate for the goal statements you've created. Make notes so you can revisit them later.

☑ WEEK 2

Block Out Time to Network

IN ORDER TO PERFORM like the successful exceptional networkers in the original six degrees of separation study, you might actually need to change some behaviors. There are four steps to changing a behavior: want it, learn it, try it, and live it. You were motivated to buy this book because you wanted to learn how to do this thing called "networking" more effectively. Congratulations! You've accomplished step one.

Having determined that you want the information, step two is to learn it. That involves actually reading this book. Congratulations again! You've made it this far. Keep going!

Once you learn this information, move to step three: try it out. Reading the book is good, but executing the strategies in the book is better. This is not a book that should just sit on your bookshelf. For the next twelve months, keep it on your desktop to remind you every day of the reason you bought it in the first place. The true purpose of this book is to keep you working on your business by implementing the fifty-two strategies to network your business effectively and efficiently.

This is not a book that should just sit on your bookshelf.

After you begin trying out the strategies, the last step in successfully implementing this material is to live it. This requires a continuing commitment on your part to execute what you learn—not just by trying one strategy each week, but by integrating your new skills in the way you conduct your business every day.

Make a written commitment to yourself and your business by blocking out time on your calendar for networking activities. You may have already started this when you wrote your networking goals. If not, find the best time in your week to focus on these strategies.

Ask yourself:

1. How much time will I dedicate to networking each week?
2. What percentage of my marketing budget will I dedicate to word of mouth?
3. How many meals each week will I eat with someone else?
4. How many new people do I want to meet each week?
5. What other methods will I use to generate new business?

Right now, your inner voice may be saying, Yeah, right. I know I need to network. But how can I manage my current business and still find time to get out and network? Shouldn't I give priority to my existing clients?

To enhance your perspective on the value and necessity of networking, let's review four primary methods for generating new business: cold calls, advertising, public relations, and networking.

Cold Calls

For most people, the term *cold call* is two "four-letter words" that raise the hairs on the backs of their necks. Many find cold-calling painful, humiliating, and frustrating, especially after they see how low a return it produces on valuable time invested.

For most people, the term *cold call* is two "four-letter words" that raise the hairs on the backs of their necks.

Think about it. How do you react when the phone rings during dinner, and it turns out to be a cold call from a salesperson? If you have caller ID, you may simply ignore the call. If you answer, you're probably not going to become a loyal customer. You may end the call by lying ("My cat's sick, and we're on the way to the vet")—or worse ("Can't you find honest work?"). One hard-nosed character we know asks the caller, "Can you hang on for a moment?" and then lays the phone down and goes back to the dinner table.

Regardless of your personal strategy for avoiding the cold caller, the point is that you go to great lengths to avoid him. Now, turn the tables. If you were the cold caller, don't you think other people might have the same reaction to you?

Advertising

Advertising, on the other hand, though typically more palatable than cold-calling, is usually more expensive. This means you probably need an advertising budget. If you dedicate money to this strategy, you expect to see results—and, truth be told, advertising will sometimes generate new business. That's why we believe in advertising. If you want to be successful, you need to advertise. But let's be honest. How many of you have gotten all the business you want through advertising? What's the return on your investment? For most of us, advertising won't produce enough new business to keep us going indefinitely. Besides, the savvy consumer tends to be wary of ads, because he or she knows that you or someone in your company wrote the content. Wouldn't you expect it to say great things about your company?

Public Relations

Next, there's public relations. PR is unpredictable and sometimes risky. Typically, you have little control over what gets written and printed, regardless of how well it does or does not represent your business. Sometimes you'll even find yourself putting out fires created by inaccurate PR. We've had tremendous success with my PR efforts. However, we've never relied on this aspect of business development alone. It is one piece of the overall marketing strategy for a business.

Networking

Finally, let's consider networking as a method for generating new business. Networking, if done strategically and exceptionally well, has the potential to generate all of your new business by word of mouth. Using networking as a strategy for generating new business truly turns it into referral marketing. This book is your week-by-week plan for building your business through referral marketing using the venues and skills of networking to make it happen.

> **Using networking as a strategy for generating new business truly turns it into referral marketing.**

Most businesses have a marketing plan that includes advertising. We are not opposed to advertising; most businesses need it to survive. However, we think you should plan your networking activities the same way you plan your other marketing activities. An effective networking plan should be part of your overall marketing strategy.

Advertising costs money. Networking, on the other hand, mostly costs time. Although it takes time and sales to make the money you need for your advertising, it's important to consider the time you devote to networking as time spent on marketing. It's part of your marketing budget. You don't need to spend a lot of money, but you have to devote time in order to cultivate the relationships necessary for generating referrals.

So just how much time do we recommend you set aside? Based on several studies conducted by BNI over the years, 52 percent of all business professionals spend four hours or less each week on their networking activities. We don't believe that's nearly enough to get you into the 29% or keep you there. In contrast, 27 percent of all businesspeople spend eight hours or more each week. We believe that the 27 percent are closer to getting it right. If sales are only part of your job responsibility, then eight hours a week seems appropriate. On the other hand, if sales represent most of your job responsibility, you need to be spending much more than eight hours a week on them. Networking is ultimately about generating referrals over time for your company. If you want to build a referral-based business, and most of your job involves sales, then your networking efforts should represent more than half of your time (yes, over twenty hours a week).

Effective networking is not just socializing, nor is it simply attending meetings. It's about building connections and relationships. That takes time. Don't feel guilty about spending time on this activity—assuming that you are truly "working" the process. The time and energy you spend on these efforts are part of your sales and marketing program. Set aside the time necessary to be successful. Those who live within six degrees of anyone in the world certainly take the time to practice networking.

Week 2 Action

OK, you know networking is the way you want to grow your business. And you know you have to want it, learn it, try it, and live it in order to change your behavior and reap the rewards. So, living it requires physically blocking out time in your schedule for networking activities. Your task this week is to do exactly that. Stop! Yes, right now! Get your PDA or calendar and schedule time to network this week.

Commit to spending enough time on your networking activities every week. Again, four hours is not enough. Seven is a good number to shoot for. If your primary job responsibility is sales, then you should be spending over twenty hours a week on this activity. You don't have to start with that many hours right away, but build up to it over time as you are implementing this weekly plan. For a while, however, you do need to track the time you're spending to ensure that you are investing enough time at it to make a difference. We suggest you color-code your calendar to track your networking efforts.

After a while, this systematic planning should have you spending the appropriate amount of time each week on activities that directly impact your networking—not just attending meetings, but all the things related to making and keeping connections and relationships with your referral sources and associates. Commit to how much time you will spend now to start this process. Plan on increasing that time over the next month or two until you hit your optimum. Then, spend that time focusing on the activities that we talk about throughout this book—working on your networking program and building your business.

☑ WEEK 3

Profile Your Preferred Client

WHO ARE YOUR PREFERRED, IDEAL CLIENTS? You know, the ones who make you smile all the time. With any luck, these are the same people who put good money in your pocket because you fit their needs to a tee. Imagine what your business would be like if you had a Rolodex filled with only the people and businesses you most like to work with. If most or all of your clients were like them, you'd be one happy camper, wouldn't you? You'd not only be making a good living, but you'd be creating a remarkable life as well.

> **Imagine what your business would be like if you had a Rolodex filled with only the people and businesses you most like to work with.**

Week 3 Action

For this strategy, your task is to profile that preferred client. This not only directs you toward the diverse people you need to meet, but it also helps to mold and clarify your message—that is, how you describe your business when you introduce yourself to someone in a networking encounter.

Profiling your preferred client means taking a hard look at what makes that organization or individual a perfect fit for you. It's not that you won't take other clients, of course, but this particular type of client is your absolute favorite on many levels. Perhaps this is a client that you wish to have, yet don't seem to have many of right now.

As with the previous strategies, this one involves asking yourself some probing questions. For example: Why are you a perfect match? What does your preferred client need that you supply? What problems does this client have that you can solve better than any of your competitors?

To make this task more concrete, let's look at an actual example of a specific preferred client profile contributed by Neal, a career/life coach:

> Women in transition (divorced, widowed, or empty-nester), mid-40s+, Westmorland or Allegheny county, currently employed, unhappy with their work or life situation, no kids at home, household income over $50,000, college graduate, home owner, with a valid driver's license.

On the next page is a preferred client worksheet for you to complete. Notice that it focuses on the demographic elements of your preferred client. The main objective of this exercise is to be as specific as possible. You can be much more effective at networking your business when you're able to profile your preferred client to the people who are listening to your message. This gives the listener more information and opens the mind's eye to his personal Rolodex, visually matching the people he knows against your specific profile. When a listener identifies a match, there's a good chance you'll get a referral.

In creating your specific profile, please don't limit yourself to the elements in this abbreviated list. Be sure to consider all elements that apply to you. Your specific profession might determine what elements you should consider. We're sure that this list can be expanded, depending on the preferred client profile that you design.

WORKSHEET FOR PROFILING YOUR PREFERRED CLIENT

Business-to-Consumer Clients	Business-to-Business Clients
Gender	Location
Family Structure	Number of Employees
Marital Status	Years in Business
Household Income	Specialty or Type of Business
Location	Size of Company (Revenue)
Education	Number of Departments
Children/No Children	Industry
Home Owner or Renter	Public or Private
Other	Other

☑ WEEK 4

Recruit Your Word-of-Mouth Marketing Team

ONCE YOU UNDERSTAND and can describe for others your preferred client, you can begin to pursue those prized catches with the help of your own personal word-of-mouth (WOM) marketing team. As a verb, *market* means to sell or offer to sell. A marketing team's primary function is to get you more business. In the six degrees study, these people were most likely the primary ones that the participants turned to in order to complete the task of the study.

With that in mind, you should be very selective as to whom you invite to become a member of your personal WOM marketing team. You have full control over this decision. Business owners refer to these folks as "evangelists," "apostles," or "influencers." (They've also been called "E. F. Huttons," after the financial company of the same name, which was sold to Shearson Lehman/American Express in 1985. Years ago the firm famously ran a series of commercials that featured two people chatting about their stock brokerages. Amid the noise of crowds and traffic, one person would say, in effect, "My broker is E. F. Hutton, and E. F. Hutton said . . ."

At that, all noise would suddenly cease as everyone stopped and turned to listen. The slogan "When E. F. Hutton talks, people listen" became something of a pop-culture phenomenon. But we digress.)

Be very selective as to whom you invite to become a member of your personal WOM marketing team.

Regardless of your choice of label, these individuals will help create buzz in the community about your business, because they believe in you, your business, and your product or service. They also (1) know you very well; (2) really like you; and (3) trust you implicitly. And when they talk, a lot of people listen (hence the "E. F. Hutton" tag). They will be the walking and talking marketing ambassadors for your business.

Who constitutes your strongest WOM team? Look for people who can provide unsolicited testimonials to help promote your business. Occasionally, these are folks who have experienced your services firsthand. Regardless, they are influential people whose recommendations and testimonials carry great weight with your preferred clients and, of utmost importance, they are willing to establish a reciprocal referral relationship with you.

Taking it one step further, consider who influences the influencer. These are people who have the undivided attention of, and serve as trusted advisors to, those who influence others. Most importantly, the members of your word-of-mouth marketing team are in touch with your preferred client on a regular basis—but for a different reason than yours. This commonality allows for referrals to flow naturally and continually back and forth.

To summarize, here are the most important criteria for your WOM team members:

1. They need to be in front of your preferred client on a regular basis, but for a different reason than yours.
2. They know you well, like you a lot, and trust you implicitly.
3. They are influential enough that others will listen to what they say.
4. If possible, they have firsthand experience with your products or services.

Here are examples of successful WOM teams (assuming that all of the above criteria have been met) for two different businesses:

- Financial advisor

   Preferred client profile: Woman in transition, 40+ years old, income of $50K+, makes household decisions, has expendable cash, lives in Westmorland or Allegheny county, college graduate, home owner, willing to drive for services

   Potential WOM team members: Career/life coach, divorce attorney, personal CPA, mediator

- Commercial carpet cleaner

   Preferred client profile: Commercial business with multiple locations, located in high-rise buildings of more than three stories, 25+ employees, 100-mile radius, $1 million in revenue, service industry

   Potential WOM team members: Commercial real estate agent, office equipment rental, window cleaners, corporate professional organizers

In searching for your WOM team, don't take just anyone. Great companies know how to keep looking for the right people— people who will help their enterprise succeed. You're no different. If you wish to become a great company, be selective and build strong relationships based on integrity and trust. Don't settle for less. Set your sights very high. The payoff to you will be far greater than you can imagine right now. Always remember: It's an honor for someone to be on your word-of-mouth marketing team.

Week 4 Action

Your task for this week: Identify three of these influential people within your network to serve on your WOM team.

1. _____
2. _____
3. _____

Please note that we address some crucial actions to perform with these key people in several strategies later in the book, such as Week 5 ("Give to Others First"), Week 15 ("Be a Value-Added Friend"), and Week 28 ("Host a Purposeful Event").

☑ WEEK 5

Give to Others First

THIS STRATEGY TOUCHES on one of the cornerstones in our philosophy about business networking excellence. Giving to others is not only an essential networking technique; it is a fundamental ethic.

The BNI network sums it up well with its trademarked two-word mantra: Givers Gain. We believe that no other two words in the English language capture so vividly, accurately, and simply the power and potential of networking at its best. If you forget every other strategy in this book (don't worry; you won't!), remember: give to others first.

> **Givers Gain. We believe that no other two words in the English language capture so vividly, accurately, and simply the power and potential of networking at its best.**

You may ask, "How do I generate referrals to other people?" Or you may say, "I get a lot of referrals from that caterer, but I'm not sure what I have to give back to him." You're not alone in these concerns. We hear them all the time from business owners and professionals who are learning the networking ropes. So let's get into the "why" and "how" details of giving referrals.

Why give to others first? The reason is simple. In order for any relationship to develop and stand the test of time, it must be beneficial to both parties, and both parties must give to the relationship.

Think about it. What's one of the most valued commodities in business? Time! No one can stand the thought of wasting time, because there's never enough of it. So, if it turns out that a relationship is only one-sided, what has been wasted? Valuable time. (OK, sometimes a lot of money, blood, sweat, and tears as well.)

By giving to others first, you take the initial step in building two-way, win-win networking relationships. You're being proactive and positive. You're leading by example, modeling the behavior you hope others will adopt.

On to the "how." Begin by understanding the phenomenal value of your network. It's a gold mine. It's a treasure chest of talents, skills, and knowledge. It holds the power to help people you care about in more ways than either you or they can imagine.

Now, look at who's holding the keys to that treasure chest: you! That's right. You are the gatekeeper to the resources locked inside your network. Think about what that means—for you, for your network, even for lots of people you haven't even met yet.

You are the gatekeeper to the resources locked inside your network.

As cartoon character Charlie Brown would say, "Good grief!" When others are experiencing grief, you can do them good. In other words, thanks to your network, you are in a position to be a problem solver.

You often hear people talk about their problems. Maybe they're complaining about their car, or telling you how they were late for a meeting because their water heater emptied onto their basement floor, or grumbling about how they hate getting hit with a big surprise tax bill at the end of the year. Statements like these from people in your life are really opportunities for you to help them solve problems.

You might not be equipped to take a direct role in, say, fixing a car, installing a new hot-water heater, or preparing a tax return, but listening for these problem-solving opportunities positions you to give referrals to people in your network.

One way to give to others first involves the Boy/Girl Scout motto. Do you know it? That's right: "Be prepared." You need to be prepared when someone you know expresses a problem that can be addressed by someone on your marketing team. Be prepared to talk about the benefits of your colleague's business, and give the person your colleague's business card.

If you become the "go-to person," people will seek you out for help, thus providing you the opportunity to activate your network as a true giver.

A second way to become an active giver in your network is to position yourself as the gatekeeper to a tremendous resource of services. If you become the "go-to person," people will seek you out for help, thus providing you the opportunity to activate your network as a true giver. One successful strategy that we recommend is to compose a letter and send it out to your client list several times a year. If it's more convenient and appropriate, you could send out a quick e-mail to your database, but send it at least once a year as hard copy, just to stand out from everyone else who's e-mailing your clients. Here's a sample letter:

Dear _____ :

I really believe in the process of referrals, and so part of the service I provide is to be sure to refer my clients and associates to other qualified businesspeople in the community.

Attached is a list of areas in which I know very credible, ethical, and outstanding professionals. If you're looking for a professional in a specific area that I've listed, please feel free to contact me. I will be glad to put you in touch with the people I know who provide these services.

Sincerely,

_____

Notice that this letter lists only professions, not names and phone numbers. The purpose is to engage your clients to contact you so you can put the referral and the contact together. Your goal is to build relationships, not just become a glorified phone book. Implementing this strategy helps you become known as an effective networker, a gatekeeper, and an honest giver. Along the way, you also build your credibility throughout the community.

One person we know used this letter strategy with all his clients (and prospects) four times in the first year. After the third time, the floodgates opened, and he received responses every time he sent it out. Today, he no longer needs to send out the letter several times a year, because he has finally attained the reputation of being a giver and a gatekeeper. People come to him because they know he knows many businesspeople in the community.

The importance of becoming a gatekeeper is huge if you seek to grow your business with word-of-mouth marketing. It's a strategy that gets people to not only contact you for a referral, but also open up a dialogue with others about what your business does and how you can help them. This, in turn, leads to more business with existing clients and more new business with prospects.

In addition, the people on your list of professions will work hard to reciprocate and send people your way. In time, even they will begin to come to you when they need someone to help solve a problem. (Be sure to copy your letter to each professional represented on that list, letting her know that you're going to be sending business her way.)

This one technique is a "touch point" that puts you in contact with your clients, prospects, and your word-of-mouth marketing team in a way that fosters the dynamics of a giving relationship that benefits all parties. You have something they need: referrals and contacts. Allow this to open the door for reciprocal sharing and giving. You'll be amazed at how much more business you can do with each other as a result.

Week 5 Action

Actually, you have two tasks for this week. First, prepare yourself to give referrals to others in your network. This is really simple. Go to your nearest office supply center and buy a business card carrier. In fact, buy three. In each of these card carriers, keep at least three cards of the primary people in your network—most importantly, the members of your word-of-mouth marketing team. Keep one card carrier in your vehicle's glove compartment, one in your briefcase, and one on your desktop. Doing this prepares you to help someone on your marketing team at any time.

Your second task this week is to construct a letter similar to the sample we've provided, and then send it to your clients and throughout your network. Be sure not to include names and phone numbers of the people whose businesses you've referenced on your list.

The bonus to both of these two actions is that once the members of your marketing team catch wind of what you're doing for them, they'll turn around and want to do the same for you. The relationship is now becoming mutually beneficial—and you're taking the lead in the relationship.

☑ WEEK 6

Create a Network Relationship Database

QUICK! NAME THE ONE HUNDRED PEOPLE who have had the greatest impact on the growth of your business. Can you list them all from memory? And can you recite their birthdays and anniversaries and the names of their top one hundred contacts?

If you can do all that, you probably don't need this part of the book. In fact, you should enter show business and take your incredible memory on the road!

We're guessing that your powers of recollection are in the "mere mortal" range—like the rest of us—and that you need some tools to keep all those details straight about your business network relationships. Luckily for all of us, such tools are easily accessible—and usually for a reasonable price.

We're talking, of course, about database and contact management software. We could fill this book with the articles we've seen on the pros and cons of the software packages available to help businesspeople keep track of clients, prospects, suppliers, etc.—not to mention the hardware options. But we're not going to do that. (Sorry, techies, you're on your own!) What we will do is emphasize the importance of having a system to reliably hold the information you need about the people who make up your network.

For many years—and perhaps still for you today—the typical "system" of choice was a card-holding contraption called a Rolodex or a knockoff under some other brand name. Simple and completely no-tech, this system uses little paper cards attached to a wheel or tray that keeps them neatly in alphabetical order. Need a phone number? Flip to the person's card. It's all manual, so you actually have to write each person's information on a separate card. Very twentieth century! But they're still available, and if you hate computers, this is the way to go.

A better choice—primarily because you can store and quickly sort through a virtually unlimited volume of data—would be the aforementioned database or contact management software. These products are available on the shelves of most major office supply stores, as well as online, direct from software vendors via the Internet.

High-tech? No-tech? Whatever works. Choose the system that's best for you. You just need a way to maintain contact information on your clients, prospects, vendors, word-of-mouth marketing team members, and anyone else whose path you hope to cross again—especially those people who are most likely to be able to refer you business.

You need to keep more than just contact information, though. Your database is the place for you to record every word-of-mouth referral that you receive from your network. You'll want to record who gave you the referral, how it developed, and whether it led to any further business. You will also want to record what you had to do to turn that referral into a client.

You need to keep more than just contact information. Record every word-of-mouth referral that you receive from your network . . . who gave you the referral, how it developed, and whether it led to any further business.

Within your database, keep track of

- how specific people help you,
- what you do for them,
- how often you meet with them,
- who they want to meet, and
- other significant information that will give you a reason to connect with them (e.g., birthdays, anniversaries, names of children and significant others—whatever they share with you that you want to recall later).

In doing so, you'll begin to recognize patterns: which people tend to pass you the most referrals, and which referrals actually turn into business. Identifying those who continually pass you business helps you dedicate equal time to generating business for them. The more information you keep in your network relationship database, the easier it'll be for you to track your successes and failures and keep pace with your networking goals and relationships.

There are many excellent programs available to accomplish this strategy. One of the best known and most effective, in our opinion, is ACT! (Sage Software). It lets you record detailed prospect and customer information for almost any business, small or large, including notes, history, customer communications, contact records, and other features that can be used throughout the networking and sales process. This is a good database software system, one that we highly recommend.

A contact database only stores contacts, and although it may be low-tech, it serves its purpose. More advanced software can go a few steps further by not only storing the contacts but sorting and classifying them for ease of use. However, even many of the newest and best software and online CRM solutions are of little help in building business referral networks. The next generation of software should enable networkers to not only link up with the right referral partner, but also share databases in joint marketing efforts, cross promotions, and other networking functions. Here are some examples of how this process can work.

In today's supercompetitive environment, a business owner simply cannot afford not to use his main asset, his book of business. A CPA makes a good case study. Let's assume the CPA is already doing a good job of marketing and staying in touch with the clients in his database. A loan officer, whose business is transactional (statistically, one obtains a mortgage every three to five years), also markets regularly to her database. Now, the loan officer starts promoting the same CPA to her book of business. The CPA gets a competitive edge by gaining a warm introduction to a whole new group of prospects. To reciprocate, the CPA recommends this particular loan officer to his clients. Not only does the cost of obtaining new business drop for both, but the quality of referrals also improves because of the warm introductions. Best of all, it's done automatically, en masse, and both referral partners gain tremendously from the crosspromotion.

Another example: After closing a loan, a mortgage broker recommends to her clients a moving company on her referral partner's list. Larger mortgages also get referrals for an interior designer. The interior designer, in turn, recommends furniture stores and remodeling contractors, who close the referral circle by recommending the mortgage broker to their client lists. The key difference that makes this process so effective is automation. All the mortgage broker's referrals are made automatically, without costing her any additional time. Errors of omission do not occur; the referral always gets passed.

An excellent example of an effective CRM system can be found at www.Relate2Profit.com. This online service is a relationship management system that also connects businesses and individuals within organizations into virtual groups, allowing them to share prospect and client data (to whatever extent they feel comfortable). They may co-market, cross-market, manage joint projects, generate referrals, and collaborate. Relationship management systems like Relate2Profit.com take contact management to the next level.

They provide all the normal contact records, communication, and history processes and allow cross-marketing with other trusted people in your network. There's nothing quite like this system for people who want to facilitate collaboration among their network members.

Week 6 Action

Your task this week is to create a database that includes your most satisfied customers, professionals who are in front of your target market all the time, people who have already given you referrals, those to whom you've given referrals, and folks who naturally get business every time you get business.

☑ WEEK 7

Master the Top Ten Traits

WE'LL SAY IT AGAIN. Networking is more than just shaking hands and passing out business cards. Networking is really about building your "social capital," according to the results of a survey of more than two thousand businesspeople throughout the US, UK, Canada, and Australia, published in *Masters of Networking* (Ivan Misner and Don Morgan). The survey respondents rated most highly the traits related to developing and maintaining good relationships. Here are the top ten traits that make a master networker, ranked in order of their importance as judged by the respondents. Do you think that the elite 29% of the population share many of these traits? We believe they do! Which do you possess?

Top Ten Traits of a Master Networker

1. Timely follow-up on referrals. This was ranked as the number-one trait of successful networkers. If you present an opportunity—whether it's a simple piece of information, a special contact, or a qualified business referral—to

someone who consistently fails to follow up successfully, it's no secret that you'll eventually stop wasting your time with this person. Following up with what you say you're going to do, when you say you're going to do it, builds your credibility and trust with your network.

2. Positive attitude. A consistently negative attitude makes people dislike being around you and drives away referrals; a positive attitude makes people want to associate and cooperate with you. When you are positive, you're like a magnet (see Week 14). People want to be around you and will send their friends, family, and associates to you. Positive attitudes are contagious. Being positive contributes to your determination, internal motivation, and ultimate business success.

3. Enthusiasm/motivation. Think about the people you know who get the most referrals. They're the people who show the most motivation, right? It's been said that the best sales characteristic is enthusiasm. To be respected within our networks, we at least need to sell ourselves with enthusiasm. Once we've done an effective job of selling ourselves, we can reap the reward of seeing our contacts sell us to others. That's motivation in and of itself! Enthusiasm aligns well with a positive attitude. Enthusiastic and motivated people make things happen for them—and for the people they know.

4. Trustworthiness. When you refer one person to another, there is no doubt that you're putting your personal and professional reputation on the line. You have to be able to trust your referral partner and be trusted in return. Neither you nor anyone else will refer a contact or valuable information to someone who can't be trusted to handle it well. Trust, as we have been taught, is earned. It develops over time and throughout the life span of a relationship. Trust can never be taken lightly, because it plays such a huge role in your credibility.

5. Good listening skills. Our success as networkers depends on how well we can listen and learn from the people in our network. The faster you and your networking partner learn what you need to know about each other, the faster you'll establish a valuable relationship. Listening for the needs and problems of others can also position you to engage the services of the people you know. Many distractions can get in the way of listening well to each other. Communicating well takes focus and effective listening.

6. Commitment to networking 24/7. Master networkers are never formally off duty. (Well, maybe when they're asleep.) Networking is so natural to them that they can be found networking in the grocery checkout line, at the doctor's office, and while picking the kids up from school—as well as at business mixers and networking meetings. Master networkers take advantage of every opportunity that's presented to them on a daily basis. They operate in the "Givers Gain" mind-set and are first and foremost looking for opportunities for the people in their network.

7. Gratitude. Gratitude is sorely lacking in today's business world. Expressing gratitude to business associates and clients is just another building block in the cultivation of relationships that will lead to increased referrals (see Week 19 Strategy). People like to refer others to business professionals who go above and beyond. Thanking others at every opportunity will help you stand out from the crowd. Expressing sincere gratitude to the people who will one day be there to help you is not just a courtesy—it's the right thing to do.

8. Helpfulness. Helping others can be done in a variety of ways, from simply showing up to help with an office move to clipping a useful and interesting article and mailing it to an associate or client. Master networkers keep their eyes and ears open for opportunities to advance other people's

interests. They offer to help others whenever they can, because they authentically want to help. It's as simple as that. Master networkers get joy out of helping other people succeed.

9. Sincerity. Friendliness without sincerity is like a cake without frosting. You can offer the help, the thanks, the listening ear, but if you aren't sincerely interested in others, it will show— and they'll know it! Those who have developed successful networking skills convey their sincerity at every turn. One of the best ways to develop this trait is to give your undivided attention to the individual with whom you're developing a referral relationship. Don't multitask when you're on the phone; stop browsing the Web, balancing your checkbook, and shining your shoes. When you multitask, nothing gets your full attention, and everything suffers in some way; besides, people can tell when you're not all there. Make eye contact when you're speaking to them in person. Sincerely show that you care, and give your complete attention to the individual in front of you.

10. Dedicated to working one's network. As mentioned previously, it's not net-sit or net-eat—it's net-WORK, and master networkers don't let any opportunity to work their networks pass them by. They manage their contacts with contact management software, organize their e-mail address files, and carry their referral partners' business cards along with their own. They set up appointments to get better acquainted with new contacts and learn as much about them as possible, so they can truly become part of one another's networks.

Do you see the common thread in these ten points? You may also notice that we elaborate further on most of these traits throughout this book. That's how strongly we feel that these traits impact your ability to get into the 29% of the population and your overall networking success. You can also see that they all tie in to proactive, long-term relationship building, not to stalking prey for the immediate big kill. People who take the time to build their social capital are the ones who will have new business referred to them over and over. The key is to build mutually beneficial business relationships. Only then will you succeed as a master networker.

Build mutually beneficial business relationships.

Week 7 Action

You'll be relieved to know that your task is not to master all ten traits of a master networker by the end of the week. No, this week we want you simply to take a brief inventory of your current skills, abilities, habits, and attitudes, and see where you stand on the network mastery scale. On the following worksheet, rate your level of mastery in each of the ten key areas.

Master Networker Trait	Never	Rarely	Sometimes	Usually	Always
1. I follow up.	—	—	—	—	—
2. I have a positive attitude.	—	—	—	—	—
3. I am enthusiastic and motivated.	—	—	—	—	—
4. I am trustworthy.	—	—	—	—	—
5. I listen well.	—	—	—	—	—
6. I network 24/7.	—	—	—	—	—
7. I thank people.	—	—	—	—	—
8. I enjoy helping people.	—	—	—	—	—
9. I am sincere.	—	—	—	—	—
10. I work my network.	—	—	—	—	—
Number checked	—	—	—	—	—
Level of mastery (multiply)	x 1	x 2	x 3	x 4	x 5
Subtotals	—	—	—	—	—

Total score (add all 5 columns) ____

If your total score is 50, you can close the book now, pour yourself a glass of champagne, stand in front of the mirror, and drink a toast to the master networker. If your score is 10, you'll have to settle for a glass of water and a sandwich, because you've got work to do. But if you're like most of us, you're somewhere between 20 and 40 on the network mastery scale—pretty good in some areas, not so great in others.

Make a note of the traits where you need the most improvement. As you advance through the weekly strategies in this book, refer back to this part and think about how applying each strategy can help you improve in these areas. This will help you identify which strategies can do you the most good in strengthening your networking skills.

Remember, you don't have to follow these weekly strategies in the order we've used in this book. If you see a strategy further along that can help you strengthen a skill you consider weak, jump ahead to it and give it your full attention. You may find this the fastest way to get your network really working for you.

One further suggestion: Make a note to yourself to revisit the Week 7 Strategy when you finish the book. Take the self-assessment test again. If you've taken the strategies to heart and put a good effort into applying them to your networking activities, you'll be surprised at how much closer you've come to being a master networker and securing your footing in the elite 29% of the population who actually are separated by six degrees from anyone else in the world.

SECTION TWO
EXPAND YOUR NETWORK

SECTION TWO PRESENTS WEEKLY STRATEGIES 8–14. Here we build on the foundation you laid for your "networking home" in Section One by focusing on populating your network.

Obviously, you need people—but you're not going to bring just anyone into your network. Moreover, your choice of people will not be personal (usually). Rather, your business and networking goals and strategies will guide you in selecting those individuals who are most likely to be a good fit.

Remember, you're not engaged in social networking here. This is strictly about business—your business and their business. Before we go shake some hands, here's a quick overview of where we're headed in Section Two.

The Week 8 Strategy ("Diversify Your Contacts") points out that most of us spend our time with people very much like ourselves. We tend to attract people who share the same values, beliefs, education, socioeconomic status, and other characteristics. In this strategy, you're asked to look beyond your normal network and find people who are different from you to broaden and diversify your network.

The Week 9 Strategy ("Meet the RIGHT People") starts off by asking you to consider who really knows about your business, who doesn't know about your business, and who should know about your business. This strategy helps you realize that there is a fundamental difference between a "contact" and a "connection."

The Week 10 Strategy ("Reconnect with People from the Past") gives a great example of how reconnecting with people from earlier in your life can sometimes open new doors for your business.

In Week 11's Strategy ("Talk to Your Family"), you begin to learn how to add depth to the conversations you have with the people who are potentially your biggest fans: your family members. Many people find that when they begin to look at individuals in their family as potential resources for networking their business, new opportunities reveal themselves.

The Week 12 Strategy ("Stop Being a Cave Dweller") stretches you out of your comfort zone by luring you beyond the safety of your cave and into the fields and meadows of active networking. This strategy will help cure you of "cave dweller syndrome"—a condition that can cause permanent business damage.

Week 13's Strategy ("Join a Web-Based Networking Group") expands your network into the realm of international exposure through online networking groups and systems.

Finally, our Week 14 Strategy ("Become Magnetic") demonstrates the importance of becoming "magnetic" with respect to networking. Magnetic people attract other people to them—and this strategy clearly demonstrates its significance.

Expanding and diversifying your network is vital if you want your business to thrive. Ultimately, it brings more people to you, lets more of them know about your business, and promotes the benefits of your business to a broader audience. So get out of your cave, meet new people, and turn on your magnetism!

☑ WEEK 8

Diversify Your Contacts

IT'S BEEN SAID THAT MOST PEOPLE know between two hundred and three hundred people. "Isn't that plenty for my network?" you might ask. "Why should I expand? Won't I dilute my efforts if I spread myself too thin, trying to keep up with so many more people?"

These may seem like good questions, but the concept underlying this strategy is stepping outside your comfort zone to meet people who are different from you. By doing so, you expose yourself and your business to people you might not have otherwise met, simply because they are not within your everyday circle of contacts.

A major key to success in building a powerful business network is diversity. Yet, it's natural for us to be attracted to people much like ourselves. People tend to cluster and congregate based on education, age, race, professional status, and other characteristics. We connect with people based on shared interests and spend time with those who have experiences or perspectives similar to ours. Most of our friends and associates know one another as well, and we find ourselves associating with the same circle of friends.

A major key to success in building a powerful business network is diversity.

The problem is that when you surround yourself with people who have similar contacts, you may find it hard to connect with new people or companies with whom you want to do business. If you limit yourself to that one circle of friends and colleagues, your business's exposure will be finite—limited to that same circle of associates, and the people they know. This can be a recipe for the slow and painful death of your business.

But think about the untapped world beyond the security of your circle of close contacts. What business opportunities could you be missing, simply because you're not connected in those circles? A diverse business network increases the chances of including connectors, or linchpins, in your network. Linchpins are people with a variety of interests that make them part of more than one network. This lets them serve as "bridges" between two or more groups of people with different interests and contacts.

Diversifying helps you locate these connectors between clusters of people. According to Wayne Baker, author of the book *Achieving Success Through Social Capital*, "Linchpins . . . are the gateways between clumps."[1] And "by linking diverse clumps, [linchpins] provide the shortcuts that convert a big world into a small one."[2] In other words, linchpins are the folks who create shortcuts across "clumps" or groups of people. Those who completed the task in the six degrees study obviously knew some linchpins. The best way to increase the number of linchpins in your network is to develop a diverse network, not a homogeneous one. The more diverse the network, the more likely that it will include overlapping connectors or linchpins that link people together in ways you never would have imagined. When it comes to business networking, you never know who people know.

**When it comes to business networking,
you never know who people know.**

One of the problems in understanding this concept is a built-in bias that many people have about networking with individuals outside their normal frame of reference. Our biases cause us to leave money on the table every day by blinding us to opportunities that are right in front of us. When you allow yourself to see through your biases and open your world to those outside your well-defined box, the possibilities are astounding. Here's a great example from a recent BNI meeting, where one of the most profitable referrals we've ever seen passed came from—brace yourself—a Mary Kay consultant!

Our biases cause us to leave money on the table every day.

How did it happen? Well, the Mary Kay consultant was giving a facial at a woman's home in West Los Angeles. As the consultant worked, the customer's husband walked by several times with a sheet of paper, grumbling and cursing under his breath. Finally his wife asked, "What's wrong, honey?"

The husband said, "I gotta fire this graphic design outfit. They're doing a horrible job. The problem is, I need someone to take over the project quickly."

Hearing this, the Mary Kay consultant turned to the woman's husband and said, "Gee, I know a great graphic designer. I think I have his card right here." She opened her business card file. "I'm going to see him tomorrow morning. Would you like me to give him your card and have him call you?"

"Absolutely," replied the husband.

The Mary Kay consultant made the connection, and the graphic designer got the job. Here's the kicker: the husband was a movie producer. The graphic design work was for his new movie. The referral turned into a six-figure contract, and the designer did such a great job that he got the producer's next movie project as well.

The moral here is that you don't know who "they" know. All too frequently we see people with built-in, self-defeating prejudices. They just don't want to do business with "this type" of business professional or "that kind" of salesperson or—heaven forbid—a cosmetics consultant. People who think this way just don't get it. The secret is to have truly diverse networks in which the people have only one thing in common: they're good at what they do. In the end, that's all that really counts. For the people who are truly successful at networking, it's all that ever counts.

In networking, someone you don't have a lot in common with could be a connector between you and a whole world of people you might not otherwise be able to meet. The more diverse your network, the more likely you are to find valuable linkages between people like you and people unlike you. The more of these linkages you can make, the stronger your network can be—and the broader your opportunities.

If you wish to build a powerful business network, branch out. Build a diverse network of professional contacts that includes people who don't look like you, sound like you, speak like you, or share your background, education, or history. The only thing they should have in common with you and others in your network is that they should be really good at what they do. Create a network like that, and you'll have a network that can help you succeed at anything.

Week 8 Action

This week, find yourself a networking mixer that you can attend within the month. Put it on your schedule. While you're at that mixer, use it as an opportunity to begin to diversify your network. Introduce yourself to someone you don't know. Look for an individual who is different from you and your typical contacts in culture, race, profession, age, gender, ability, interests, or beliefs. If you choose to develop this relationship, find out about the person's network. In time, ask this new friend to take you into his or her circle of contacts.

It's a big world out there. We can benefit by connecting with it—if only we remove our blinders and have the courage to say hi to a stranger (ignoring Mom's voice in our head: "Don't speak to strangers!"). Remember, the people in your network whom you now know and like were once strangers.

☑ WEEK 9

Meet the RIGHT People

EFFECTIVE NETWORKING is not simply about meeting a lot of people. And it's certainly not about seeing how many business cards you can hand out in a ninety-minute time span. More importantly, it's about meeting the right people at the right time for the right reason. Ultimately it's about knowing the difference between a "contact" and a "connection."

In this context, a contact is someone you know, but with whom you haven't fully established a strong relationship. A connection is someone who knows you, likes you, and trusts you, because you've taken the time to establish credibility with him.

Master networkers know that a good contact isn't necessarily a good connection. One of the most important things we've learned is that it's not what you know, or even who you know—it's how well you know them and how well they know you that really counts in building a powerful network.

It's not what you know, or even who you know—it's how well you know them and how well they know you that really counts in building a powerful network.

This means that your network must not only be broad; it must also be deep. Unfortunately, most people focus more on broad than on deep. They concentrate on making more and more contacts, hoping to find that one special person who'll solve their business needs this month. These people collect a lot of cards, but they never fully understand the true meaning of networking.

Have you ever felt that the time you spent networking was wasted? If you have, it's time to make a change. Most people who feel this way are approaching networking for all the wrong reasons. They expect that if they invest time and money at a networking event, they'll inevitably leave the event with a new client or two. We hate to be the bearers of bad news, but that expectation is unrealistic and will eventually cause those people to give up on networking altogether. Don't be one of them!

A networking event is not—we repeat, *not*—designed to bring strangers together for the purpose of referring themselves to one another. Why would you refer yourself to someone you barely know? A typical networking event is designed to have people who don't know one another meet and mingle.

Meet and mingle? What does that actually mean? It means meeting new people (see Week 8 Strategy) and mingling (going from person to person). But for a networking event to be fully productive for you, you must meet the right people for the right reasons. Meeting the right people will make a positive impact on your business and give you a high return on your networking investment.

If you're networking to expand your network, to develop a reliable and effective network, it's important to keep in mind depth as much as breadth. What do we mean by this? When you need to rely on others to help you out (promote your program to their client base, or cross-market your products), you need to have already done the work of strengthening the relationships with your connections, well in advance of expressing your need or request. This is critical.

So, at networking events, who are the right people to meet? Consider two types of individuals: those serving your preferred clients (Week 3 Strategy) and those who have the potential to help you meet your business goals.

Let's begin by looking at those who serve the same preferred client as you. "Hey, aren't those folks likely to be my competitors?" you might wonder. Not necessarily. Consider two examples.

- Lorraine is a real estate agent whose preferred clients are retired home owners or empty nesters with assets over $1 million, who love to travel, are country club members, and seriously pamper their pets. Other suppliers for their services might include high-end salons and spas, professional landscapers, financial advisors, country club owners, travel agents, home-cleaning service providers, and pet resorts.

- Tanya is the owner of a direct-mail company that targets colleges and universities. When Tanya could not determine who else serviced the decision makers at the university, her marketing coach asked her if she had a current client in that preferred market. She said yes. Then she was asked, "How well do you know her? Will she take your call? Would she grant you thirty minutes of her time?" Tanya emphatically replied, "Yes!" Her coach then suggested that she schedule a purposeful meeting (Week 23 Strategy) and sit down with her to pick her brain on who she grants her time to and who else supports her needs.

Your preferred clients have many suppliers for their needs, and it could be in your best interest to connect and build relationships with those other suppliers. The answers to the questions that were asked of Tanya helped direct her to the people she should be searching for while networking. You can gain the same benefit by having a similar conversation with one of your preferred clients and asking questions like these:

"Who else solves your daily problems?"

"Who do you allow in the door?"

"What companies do you call on when you need [product]?"

"Whom do you trust when it comes to helping you [type of service]?"

When you're networking, focus on meeting these people, because they probably have a Rolodex or PDA filled with the names of your preferred clients. When you're at networking events, look for name tags that fit specific professional categories you're seeking to cultivate. Ask, "Who's your preferred client?" If you meet a professional who services your preferred client—and you like the individual as a person—consider this the first step in building a new relationship. If you build a trusting and giving relationship with someone who provides services for your preferred client market, it stands to reason that your referral potential will increase dramatically. Remember that in a true triwin (that's win-win-win) relationship, that person's referral potential will also increase, and the client will get the best service possible.

The other types of people that you want to meet while networking are those who can help you meet your business goals. If you haven't set business goals, you need to make that your top priority this week! If you do have business goals, don't let them collect dust on your corkboard or get covered up in your drawer. Make it a point to review them each month. Choose a goal. The big question you need to ask yourself is "Who do I need to meet to help me accomplish this goal?"

It's tough to make it alone in today's competitive business environment. Even the biggest sports stars or presidential candidates can't reach their goals alone—so why should we try to go it alone?

Let's say that one of your business goals this year is to write an article for a local business paper. How would you network your way to achieving that goal?

First, start reading the paper. Who writes the articles? Who writes for other papers in your area? Who are their editors? Get the word out to your own network. There's a fair chance that it includes someone who can put you in contact with the right individual. Let it be known that you want to meet writers, editors, and others working for these papers, to gain insight and knowledge into how they accomplished something that you aspire to do—and that you do not intend to sell to these people.

Then look for networking events sponsored by these publications. You'll probably find staff members there providing support. Be sure to meet and speak with the right people—professionals connected to the publication—again, with the intention of learning how to write an article for your local business paper. By networking with the people who can guide you, you're well on your way to achieving your goal.

Another example of this strategy is to think of the people involved in the six degrees of separation study. They had a goal to achieve . . . to get a package to a specific person that they did not know. We would venture to suspect that the successful people in the study began by scouring their network for the right people who could help them accomplish this goal. Choosing anyone and everyone would have increased the links along the way . . . which was obviously the strategy of the 71% of the people who never connected at all.

In summary, remember: When you're considering asking someone in your personal network for a favor, ask yourself whether she's a contact or a connection. Avoid the trap of having unrealistic expectations of your network, such as support that your contacts may feel you don't deserve. You have to earn the loyalty and engagement of your referral sources. Your current goal has two parts: (1) to meet the right people, and (2) to develop deep relationships with them over time.

Week 9 Action

This week, your task is to complete the following worksheet to help you focus on who you should be meeting the next time you are at a networking event. For help in creating this list, review your preferred client profile from the Week 3 Strategy ("Profile Your Preferred Client").

Identify professions (other than your own) that serve your preferred client market:

1. _____
2. _____
3. _____
4. _____
5. _____

Identify two business goals and the individuals you might seek out for help in accomplishing each goal.

Goal #1: _____

_____

People to help you meet that goal:

1. _____
2. _____

Goal #2: _____

_____

People to help you meet that goal:

1. _____
2. _____

☑ WEEK 10

Reconnect with People from the Past

CLOSE YOUR EYES AND REMEMBER those close relationships you once had in high school, in college, in previous jobs, and in past neighborhoods. Whatever happened to those people? Are there people from the past that you haven't contacted in a while? Many of us have those people in our lives. Maybe we communicate with them twice a year (once during the holiday season, with a lengthy recap letter of highlights from the year).

These people obviously mean something to you, because otherwise you wouldn't stay in touch with them, or they with you. And if that's the case, if you asked them for help on something, they would probably do whatever they could to help you.

It's time they knew more about what's going on in your business, because you never know who they might know and how they might be able to help you. But here's a key point to remember: always offer them something in return for their help. One-sided relationships don't last long.

Jill Green, a freelance coach and trainer in the United Kingdom, offers a good example of how this strategy can work for your business:

> I was looking at a trainer's network Web site one day, when something made me search for a colleague and friend I first worked with twenty-five years ago. As young assistants and then line managers working for the same hotel company, we were part of a team who knew how to work hard and play hard! Last time I had seen Clive, some seven years before, he was an extremely successful training consultant. Then we both moved and lost touch . . . you know how that can happen. Clive was someone I respected and trusted. I wanted to find him to rekindle the friendship. I wanted to pick his brains and ask his advice about my development as a freelance coach and trainer.
>
> My search was successful—I found Clive listed, got in touch, and we reconnected in that way that old friends do. I met his partner and was delighted to be invited to their forthcoming wedding. A couple of months later, I received a call from someone who said, "You may not remember me—we met at Clive's wedding. A client of mine needs customer care training—I can't help, as my trainer is on maternity leave. Clive told me that you were just the person!" Now I was truly amazed—not just by the sequence of events—but by the fact that I didn't consider myself to be a customer care trainer! A little reflection made me realize that Clive was remembering the person he knew over twenty years ago—had added on the experience he knew I had gained since—and had given me an opportunity that was really exciting. That contract turned into over £20,000 worth of business. I learned a lot about myself, and it gave my fledgling coaching, training, and facilitation business a wonderful start.

I asked Clive for his advice and he responded by giving me a very lucrative referral. Now I know how it works. You don't need to leave these things to chance—you can truly manage your referral business![1]

Week 10 Action

Take a moment to write down a name for each category on the page that follows. During this week, call or e-mail one person on this list. Tell him you have exciting news about your business and wanted to reconnect with him to share the news. (The key is to have something really cool to share: action you've taken over the past year that has grown your business 100 percent, a new product you're about to introduce, an incredible strategic alliance you're entering into, or what-have-you.) Or follow Jill's example and ask his advice about a business matter. The more people you tell about what's going on in your business, the more positive buzz it will create on your behalf. And that's exactly what you want when you're networking your business: positive BUZZ!

People from Your Past

Neighbor _____

Phone _____

E-mail _____

Friend from a club or association _____

Phone _____

E-mail _____

College friend _____

Phone _____

E-mail _____

Work colleague _____

Phone _____

E-mail _____

Supervisor _____

Phone _____

E-mail _____

☑ WEEK 11

Talk to Your Family

WHEN WAS THE LAST TIME you talked to your brother, sister, parents, cousins, aunts, and uncles about your business? If an acquaintance asked them what you do for a living, could they tell him? For that matter, could your significant other state clearly what you do? Or would he or she say, "Your guess is as good as mine"?

When we get together with our families, most of us talk about kids, health, sports, weather, vacations, memories, neighbors, family friends, politics, religion, problems, and other personal matters. Rarely does the conversation center on our businesses or our work (unless, of course, you have a family-owned business). Families are the center of our social networks. Because of this, the conversations are socially oriented.

Family members are usually the people who know us best. They understand the core of who we are and what life dealt us to create the adults we are today. They support our endeavors and celebrate our successes. They are often our biggest fans. So why don't we leverage our biggest fans to help us network our business? Why do we daily leave this money sitting on the table right in front of us?

Family members are often our biggest fans. So why don't we leverage our biggest fans to help us network our business?

Suppose you have two brothers and two sisters. Of those four siblings, three are huge fans of yours (the fourth is still grumpy about that comic book you stole when you were ten). Each works at a different company and is surrounded by his or her own personal and professional networks. Remember we said that the average person knows between 200 and 300 people? This means that your three siblings together know perhaps 750 people who are not aware of your business. They know you; they love you; they trust you. So why wouldn't they refer their friends and colleagues to you? Often it's because they don't know how.

Ever heard of the "Golden Goose"? In the Brothers Grimm fairy tale of that name, it's a goose that lays golden eggs. Getting a golden egg—a great referral—is nice, but getting five golden eggs in a row from the same source is terrific. However, what you really want to do is go find the source of that never-ending supply of eggs. You want a sure thing. You want the Golden Goose. And that Golden Goose may be right next to you at the dinner table every Thanksgiving. It's quite possible that one or more of your brothers or sisters is a Golden Goose—and unaware of it.

Consider the example of Tim who works for a major federal credit union. Tim came to realize how much money he was leaving on the table and decided it was time to do something about it before someone else walked off with it. Before long he found himself at a family cookout, talking to his uncle Bob. His uncle had heard from Tim's parents about his new job and asked Tim to tell him about it.

Tim described his duties, then went on to tell about some of his firm's special savings options and other services. Then he asked his uncle how he liked his bank.

"OK, I guess," said Uncle Bob. "But they keep adding on all these fees, and I don't think it has all the services your credit union offers. Maybe I should open an account there. What do you think?"

Tim's cousins overheard the conversation, and they wanted to know more, too. By the end of the afternoon, Tim's client list had grown by six: his uncle, two cousins, a sister, and his parents! On top of that, Tim now has a Golden Goose. Uncle Bob has become a fire-breathing evangelist for the credit union, telling everyone he meets about his nephew's credit union and how much it has to offer its clients.

Week 11 Action

So . . . unless you're a CIA operative or a chicken thief, it's time to tell your family what you do. Your task this week is to schedule lunch (or a telephone call, if distance provides a challenge) with your mom, dad, sister, brother, aunt, uncle, nephew, or niece. During your lunch (or call), shift your assumptions and begin to consider the person in front of you as a potential business resource with a broad network of people you don't know. This list will give you some guidance for your meeting:

1. Tell her you want to get to know more about what she does for a living (providing she's not retired or too young to be working).

2. Ask how you can help her in her professional or business endeavors.

3. Ask about any problems she might be having at work or at home. You might know someone in your network who could help her.

4. Tell her you're trying to network your business and that you'd like her help.

5. Explain to her what you do for a living and how it benefits your clients.

6. Tell her stories about your best customers.

7. Schedule another meeting.

8. Invite her to your office so she can see for herself what you do.

Being able to help your siblings and other family members with the resources in your network not only makes you feel good, but it helps to establish you as the "go-to" person in the family whenever there is a need. This allows you to activate your network and helps many people who are important to you.

☑ WEEK 12

Stop Being a Cave Dweller

IN THE WORLD OF NETWORKING, a "cave dweller" is defined as "someone who remains in one of several confined spaces for the duration of an entire business day, day after day." Mark is a typical cave dweller. He gets up in the morning in his home cave, climbs into his mobile cave (his four-wheel-drive SUV), and speeds to his destination for the day—his office cave. He talks to the same people every day, perhaps visiting the familiar caves of a few colleagues or the same daily diner cave for lunch down the street. At the end of the day, he pilots his rolling cave back the way he came, ending up safely in his home cave, and watches his big-screen TV. Many cave dwellers, like Mark, find themselves stuck in this pattern day after day.

The problem is, networking is a contact sport. You have to get out of that cave and make contact with people!

Cave dwellers will always remain in the 71% of the population who are unsuccessful networkers because they become prisoners of their routine. They receive very little social stimulation. Many rarely leave the confines of their offices, except for the occasional lunch out with the same group of coworkers at the same corner restaurant, seeing the same waiter, and (for some) eating the same food! As far as networking goes, they have successfully created what we call a "closed network."

For someone who wants to grow and network a business, a closed network is a recipe for disaster. It limits your connections to a small, unchanging group of people—unlike an open network, which broadens your connections to a practically unlimited number of individuals. A closed network blocks out both the risk and the potential of the unfamiliar, but an open network exposes you to opportunities that you might never have seen had you remained in your cave. Which has the greater potential for business growth? Pretty obvious, isn't it?

Are you a cave dweller? If so, it's way past time to change your behavior. But we're not going to tell you it's a snap, because breaking out of your cave-bound routine will take commitment on your part. It's going to require you to venture outside your comfort zone and—take a deep breath—network! Or should we say . . . net-WORK!

Now, with your renewed commitment to networking your business, it's in your best interest to practice smart networking. Smart networking is focused and strategic. Smart networking reaps a high return on its investment of time, money, and energy. Smart networking is no longer an option for the success of your business—it's a prerequisite.

Consider these questions: If you're going to get out of your cave, where should you go to meet the right people? How often should you venture out of your cave? Should you venture out alone? What organizations should you join? You may want to take another look at the Week 3 Strategy ("Profile Your Preferred Client") as well as our Week 4 Strategy ("Recruit Your Word-of-Mouth Marketing Team"). The best networking events to attend would be those that either serve your target market or are likely to have professions represented by your marketing team. Which events are aligned with your business goals? Which networking organization or group will help you meet your business and networking goals? By choosing carefully where to venture, you increase the return on your networking investment and, in the long run, raise your comfort level outside the cave.

Rebecca, a CFP with Ameriprise Financial Services, Inc., gives us a prime example of how this strategy can have a direct impact on your business. At one point, Rebecca had all but given up on networking events, because she never seemed to get any business out of them. She saw networking as an ineffective use of her time. Most of her colleagues seemed to agree with her. In her current routine, she was not meeting new people. She had become a cave dweller.

Eventually she realized that regardless of how she felt about networking events, she still needed the visibility and the connections. Based on what she learned in a course on networking by the Referral Institute, she decided to venture out of her cave with a more strategic approach and a different mind-set. In the past, she had attended many networking events that were structured as "progressive meals": each participant sat at a table with one group of people for a while, then everyone rotated to another table. Although some like this style of networking, Rebecca found these events to be very limiting, focused mainly on helping people who found it difficult to start conversations. They didn't let her mingle freely, the way she preferred.

Rebecca is no longer a cave dweller. She regularly attends specific types of networking events that are more to her liking, and she usually achieves her goal. She goes to each event with a plan—not to find clients for herself but to form specific kinds of connections that will help her word-of-mouth marketing team. She has become a better referral partner, and yet she spends four hours less per month than before on networking—time that she turns into billable hours.

Week 12 Action

Your task this week is to venture outside your cave at least once! Talk to your best clients. Find out what networking events they attend, and ask them to take you along as their guest. Ask your word-of-mouth marketing team the same questions. Search online and in your local business paper for other community networking opportunities.

Venture outside your cave.

As a cave dweller just beginning to venture out, you'll be more comfortable attending a networking event with another person. Choose someone who knows you well, is not in your profession, and is not a cave dweller. But above all, step out of your cave, into the light. Every event you attend is another opportunity to expand and diversify your network and to help not only your own business but the businesses of those you care about. Stepping out of your cave could be the first step in moving in the direction of the 29% solution!

☑ WEEK 13

Join a Web-Based Networking Group

WHEN WE USE THE WORD *NETWORK,* people who aren't familiar with it as a marketing concept occasionally think we're referring to computers and their links to the World Wide Web. We're always glad to explain the difference and educate people about referral networking. But one day we realized that our version of the word *network* really does have a connection to today's wired-up world.

Many aspects of our lives these days, from finding health-care information to getting traffic updates, have migrated to the virtual world of the Internet—and the same thing is happening in networking. We're not really surprised by this. After all, the Internet is undeniably one of the fastest ways to exponentially increase your visibility to hundreds of thousands of people—for whatever purpose. From a business perspective, going online takes your company instantly into the international arena. Suddenly, you and your business become accessible worldwide, 24/7/365.

If you harness the power of the Internet wisely, the result can be something like putting your business networking efforts on steroids. Consider the following excerpt from *The Virtual Handshake:*

Opening Doors and Closing Deals Online, a book by David Teten and Scott Allen on building business relationships online: "Online networks are the new power lunch tables and the new golf courses for business life in the US. In the past ten years, online dating has become mainstream; 40 million Americans use online dating sites. Now businesspeople are starting to use the same family of technology to find business clients, new partners, and jobs through virtual contacts they make online."[1]

The earliest online networking sites were personal connection services, helping people reestablish old ties (long-lost friends and classmates, genealogy, etc.) or make new ones (dating and matchmaking). Today, online social networking forums such as Friendster, MySpace, and Connexion are being used more and more for business purposes. Michael Jones, cofounder and CEO of Userplane in Los Angeles, has stated that "this use of online, friend/associate-based networking will prove to be one of the most valuable business tools the Internet has yet provided."[2]

As if to prove Jones's point, AOL acquired his company in August 2006. According to Ted Leonsis, vice chairman and president, AOL Audience Business, "Userplane will expand and extend the reach and relevance of the AOL instant messaging franchise, while continuing to provide social networking audiences and specialized communities with brandable clients tailored to meet their needs."[3]

AOL says instant messaging is "one of the three most popular Internet activities in the United States—after e-mail and search—and is a key driver of user engagement."[4] In other words, the Internet has created powerful new ways for human beings to contact each other. Since these social networks are successful at bringing people together, why not consider using the same system to bring business professionals together—to design and expand networks, form partnerships, increase visibility, and dramatically increase network diversity?

There are many online business networks on the Internet today. One that we recommend is www.Ecademy.com. If you choose to join this online network, make sure to participate in the "community" in whatever way you can best develop a presence at the site. Posting on relevant bulletin boards is a great way to gain visibility, which can lead to credibility and eventually profitable business.

If you belong to a face-to-face networking group and then join an online networking group like Ecademy, consider creating a regional or national club or subcommunity for the members of your in-person group. For example, visit www.bni.ecademy.com to look at the synergy created via BNI and Ecademy. By combining the in-person networking with an online networking program, you enhance the relationships with people that you meet regularly, and you expand your networking efforts with others around the world.

Keep in mind that it's not enough just to join and get your name on the membership list. You must focus on building relationships (turning contacts into connections) with other members of the community. This is a new concept to some, but others quickly realize that they can develop a relationship with people without meeting face-to-face.

**It's not enough just to join and get your
name on the membership list.**

Be active in the community. Post topics on threads that deal with your area of expertise. Respond to postings on other threads if the subject is at all relevant to your field of expertise. The more you are "seen," the larger the number of people with whom you interact on the site, the more you're talked about, and the more visibility you will gain. One note of caution: Don't join too many of these, or you'll spread yourself too thin to build good relationships.

Another word of caution: Sometimes it's easy to get carried away with all the whiz-bang hoopla surrounding Internet developments. Never forget, however, that effective networking depends on strong, lasting relationships with trusted business professionals. Technology has made it more convenient to link with many more people—but there are no true shortcuts. Those contacts aren't terribly valuable if you don't establish trust, respect, and friendship. Networking is all about building good relationships—even online.

Week 13 Action

Time to begin pounding the keyboard—or clicking the mouse—and exploring online networking for yourself. By the end of the week, join an online networking group, and take a high-tech step toward networking your business. At the writing of this book, the three most popular business online network forums are LinkedIn.com, Ecademy.com, and Ryze.com. More than 2 million people are registered on LinkedIn, including the likes of John Kerry and Bill Gates. It's an easy system to navigate and a solid place to begin your online networking exposure.

Keep in mind that people never like to be sold to. Be cautious about your online approach, and don't let the ease of building contacts distract you from building solid relationships. And now that we've got your feet planted firmly on the ground, here are five ways to break into online networking:

1. Join one or more online networking communities with the intention of building relationships.
2. Start a blog, or write a regular column for a Web site or e-newsletter.
3. Develop an e-mail newsletter for your own company.
4. Never forget that online networking is still about building trust.
5. Understand that online networking has its own cultural norms.

We have stressed the importance of building relationships even in a "virtual" network. To build and maintain these relationships, you will need to be someone that other folks want to be around – whether in a cyberspace meeting room or while sharing a table at a business luncheon. In other words, you need to become magnetic. Our next strategy will help you do just that!

☑ WEEK 14

Become Magnetic

THERE ARE TWO PRIMARY ELEMENTS involved with this strategy. The first is your magnetism—your ability to attract people to you. The second is your approachability, the extent to which others perceive you as being open to their advances. Together, these two qualities have a lot to do with having a positive attitude, one of the Top Ten Traits of a Master Networker (see Week 7 Strategy). And together, they influence how magnetic you become for your business.

Did you know that every person has a little magnetism already inside him? It's the spinning of an atom's electrons that causes our magnetism. Since our bodies are made up of atoms with tiny spinning electrons, all of our atoms become potential magnets. Paired electrons usually cancel out each other's magnetic fields, but very powerful magnets can force some atoms to align.

A magnetic resonance imaging (MRI) machine, used in hospitals, is a perfect example of a powerful magnet. MRIs use superconducting magnets that are about twenty thousand times more powerful than Earth's magnetic field. MRI machines create a supermagnetic field capable of aligning a small percentage of the atoms in your body. This momentarily makes you a living magnet.

What if you could become a living magnet for your business? Who or what would be attracted to you?

In business, some use the term *magnetism* to mean being a center of influence. What if you could become a living magnet for your business? Who or what would be attracted to you? Being a center of influence involves positioning yourself to attract other people to you. It means becoming recognized in the community as the go-to person, the one with a broad network, the person who knows people who can solve other people's problems. That's you! Or, at least, that's who you want to become. That's who you need to be to stand out from your competition. That's who you need to be to get into and stay in the 29%.

Becoming a center of influence makes you a living magnet for your business.

A magnet's strength is related to the composition of the magnet—not necessarily the size. You've probably heard of a person having a "magnetic" personality. Perhaps you're thinking of someone like that right now. The word *magnetic* means "possessing an extraordinary power or ability to attract."[1] We tend to attract people most like ourselves in our daily encounters. You may have experienced the challenges of trying to get a group of six close friends together. Busy people attract other busy people, making it more challenging to get that group together. However, the rewards are great when the schedules align for a nice dinner or evening out.

Now let's consider the second element of becoming magnetic: your approachability factor. Scott Ginsberg, author of *The Power of Approachability*, has spent a lot of time researching the true meaning of approachability and how it affects our relationships. You may have heard of Scott. He's also known as "the Nametag Guy" (he wears a name tag everywhere he goes). He's the author of several books, and he's a professional speaker who helps people maximize their approachability, become unforgettable, and make names for themselves.

Scott emphasizes that approachability is a two-way street. "It's both you stepping onto someone else's front porch, and you inviting someone to step onto your front porch." Here are several tips we've borrowed (and modified) from Scott on how to maximize your approachability.

> **Approachability is a two-way street. "It's both you stepping onto someone else's front porch, and you inviting someone to step onto your front porch."**

1. Be Ready to Engage

When you arrive at a meeting, event, party, or anywhere many conversations will take place, prepare yourself. Be "ready to engage," with conversation topics, questions, and stories in the back of your mind, ready to go as soon as you meet someone. This will help you avoid those awkward "How's the weather?" discussions.

2. Focus on CPI

"CPI" stands for Common Point of Interest. It's an essential element in every conversation and interaction. Your duty, as you meet new people, or even as you talk with those you already know, is to discover the CPI as soon as possible. It helps establish a bond between you and others. It increases your approachability and allows them to feel more comfortable talking with you.

3. Give Flavored Answers

You've heard plenty of "fruitless questions" in your interactions with other people—questions like "How's it going?" "What's up?" or "How are you?" When such questions come up, Scott warns, don't fall into the conversation-ending trap of responding, "Fine." Instead, offer a "flavored answer": "Amazing!" "Any better and I'd be twins!" or "Everything is beautiful." Your conversation partner will instantly change her demeanor, smile, and, most of the time, inquire further to find out what made you answer that way. Why? Because nobody expects it. Not only that, but offering a true response to magnify the way you feel is a perfect way to share yourself, or "make yourself personally available" to others.

4. Don't Cross Your Arms at Networking Events

Even if it's cold, you're bored, or you're just tired and don't want to be there—don't cross your arms. It makes you seem defensive, nervous, judgmental, close-minded, or skeptical. It's a simple, subconscious, nonverbal cue that says, "Stay away." People see crossed arms, and they drift away. They don't want to bother you. You're not approachable.

Think about it. Would you want to approach someone like that? Probably not. So when you feel that urge to fold your arms across your chest, like a shield, stop. Be conscious of its effect. Then relax and do something else with your arms and hands. (There's more good advice about body language in our Week 24 Strategy: "Make First Impressions Count").

5. Give Options for Communication

Your friends, colleagues, customers, and coworkers communicate with you in different ways. Some will choose face-to-face; some will e-mail; others will call; still others will do a little of everything. Accommodate them all. Give people as many ways as you can to contact you. Make it easy and pleasant.

On your business cards, e-mail signatures, Web sites, and marketing materials, let people know they can get in touch with you in whatever manner they choose. Maybe you prefer e-mail, but what matters most is the other person's comfort and ability to communicate with you effectively. There's nothing more annoying to a "phone person" than to discover she can't get hold of you unless she e-mails you.

6. Always Have Business Cards

At one time or another you've probably been on either the telling or listening end of a story about a successful, serendipitous business encounter that ended with the phrase "Thank God I had one of my business cards with me that day!" If you recall saying something like that yourself, great! You're practicing approachability by being easy to reach.

If not, you've no doubt missed out on valuable relationships and opportunities. And it happens. People forget cards, neglect to get their supply reprinted, or change jobs. Always remember: There is a time and a place for networking—any time and any place! You just never know who you might meet.

7. Conquer Your Fear

Do you ever hear yourself saying, "They won't say hello back to me. They won't be interested in me. I will make a fool of myself"?

Fear is the number-one reason people don't start conversations—fear of rejection, fear of inadequacy, fear of looking foolish. But practice will make this fear fade away. The more you start conversations, the better you will become at it. So be the first to introduce yourself, or simply to say hello. When you take an active rather than passive role, you will develop your skills and lower your chances of rejection.

8. Wear Your Name Tag

We've heard every possible excuse not to wear name tags, and all of them can be rebutted:

"Name tags look silly." Yes, they do. But remember, everyone else is wearing one too.

"Name tags ruin my clothes." Not if you wear them on the edge of your lapel, or use cloth-safe connectors, like lanyards and plastic clips.

"But I already know everybody." No, you don't. You may think you do, but new people enter and leave businesses and organizations all the time.

"But everyone already knows me." No, they don't. Even the best networkers know there's always someone new to meet.

Your name tag is your best friend for several reasons. First of all, a person's name is the single piece of personal information most often forgotten—and people are less likely to approach you if they don't know (or have forgotten) your name. Second, it's free advertising for you and your company. Third, name tags encourage people to be friendly and more approachable.

Back to the topic of magnetism ... Scott's axiom about the common point of interest is particularly powerful for networking your business. Consider the people you know best right now. If you know them through work, they all share work with you as a CPI. If you know them through your soccer league, they share your interest in soccer. With that in mind, you could be attracting people who later—after you've built a relationship starting from this common ground—could help your business through a collaborative effort.

Remember the conversation earlier in the book about your preferred client? Remember the concept of aligning yourself with people who serve the same preferred client as you? Those people share a lot of interests with you, and attracting them to you will definitely move your business forward.

The same goes for your competitors. Believe it or not, you have a lot in common with them, too, and if you're open to acknowledging each other's strengths, you could think of opportunities for very profitable collaborations. Do you tend to avoid your competitors? You're not alone. Yet we know from experience that magnetic businesses grow on all levels—and through all kinds of CPIs and collaborations. Natural competitors can become collaborators, as long as both parties are willing.

Week 14 Action

We believe so strongly in this strategy that we have given you two tasks this week. The first is to list your top three competitors. Analyze one of them. Seriously consider his or her strengths and your strengths. What would your business look like if you were able to collaborate with one of your main competitors? What would the collaboration look like if you knew it could not fail? What would be the reaction of your customers?

Top three competitors:

1. _____

2. _____

3. _____

The second task is to list the top three people you know who are magnetic. Spend time with them over the next few months. Go with them to a networking function, and observe their interactions. Talk to them to gain their insight or uncover some of their special tips or techniques.

Top three magnetic people:

1. _____

2. _____

3. _____

You'll certainly be able to put the gems you'll get from your interactions with your top three magnetic people to good use in the next section. This is where we illustrate some tried-and-true ways to not only build your network relationships, but strengthen them into solid bonds that last—and remain profitable—for years.

SECTION THREE
GO THE EXTRA MILE

SECTION ONE WAS ALL ABOUT YOU and laying a foundation for your "networking home." Section Two took you into the processes of connecting with others to construct that home. Now we're in Section Three, where we build on those connections by purposefully strengthening your network relationships. You want to be in solid with the people who constitute your network, and vice versa. You want to be the first name that comes to mind when they scratch their heads and wonder, "Hmmm . . . Who could I go to with that problem? Who would be a good fit for that referral?"

Going the extra mile provides you several ways to stand out and be positively memorable. Weekly Strategies 15–20 focus on things that you can do to demonstrate the unforgettable value you bring to the table as a network member.

After all, we're all human, governed by the laws of human nature. Even though our networking is about business, not social relationships, you have to admit, people like people who help them. And typically, the law of reciprocity adds a sense of security to this human bond. If you help someone, he or she, in turn, wants to help you.

The strategies in this section encourage you to take the initiative in developing a relationship with someone who could be of help to you in networking your business. Let's briefly preview these strategies before diving into the details.

The Week 15 Strategy ("Be a Value-Added Friend") focuses your attention on the kind of value that you bring to the relationships you form. After all, your friends may laugh at your jokes, your neighbors might appreciate that you keep your lawn trimmed, and your pet cocker spaniel wags his tail gleefully whenever you walk into the room. The individuals in your business network, however, bring a different value scale to the party.

Week 16's Strategy ("Become a Catalyst") shows you how to be the person who makes things happen. To be successful at business networking, you can't just stand by idly and watch, waiting for someone else to act—you need to take the lead.

The Week 17 Strategy ("Find an Accountability Partner") guides you in finding a person to whom you can be accountable, responsible, answerable—for your own good. Your accountability partner is someone who cares whether—and how effectively—you execute this material and meet the goals you set for your business.

The Week 18 Strategy ("Volunteer and Become Visible") encourages you to volunteer as a way of building visibility for your business. Volunteering plays a significant role in how your business is perceived in the community—and your intentions need to be authentic.

The Week 19 Strategy ("Send a Thank-You Card") focuses on a simple but powerful two-minute activity. You may think everyone does this. Actually, few people do it—and still fewer do it effectively.

The Week 20 Strategy ("Follow Up TODAY") clarifies the significance of follow-up—timely follow-up—and its importance in pushing a relationship forward.

Keep in mind that your goal is to network your business. Going the extra mile with the people in your network not only expresses your sincerity, but it also opens the door to accept what the law of reciprocity has to offer you and your business.

☑ WEEK 15

Be a Value-Added Friend

SOUTHERN CALIFORNIA HAS MANY eucalyptus trees. They're huge—tall and lush. Yet, for all their majesty, they have a weakness, one that is not immediately apparent to the naked eye. They tend to topple over fairly easily in heavy winds. It happens almost every year. When they're uprooted and blown over by the wind, it's easy to see the reason for their instability. Their root system is broad, but not very deep at all.

We've seen some people with networks that share the weakness of those eucalyptus roots: wide, but shallow. Don't let this happen to you and your network. As we said in our Week 9 Strategy ("Meet the RIGHT People"), your network must be strong, deep, and broad. Without these three characteristics, your business is likely one day to topple over in a strong storm!

For this week's strategy, keep those eucalyptus trees in mind as we discuss your network relationships. Let's begin by focusing on the people who make up your word-of-mouth marketing team. As you get to know these people, you should make a point to "go deep." You don't want to pry or violate their privacy, of course.

Rather, as you naturally get acquainted, learn about their goals and challenges—business, personal, educational, and financial. Knowing this information will help you identify many ways that you can help them.

When you help someone meet a goal, you instantly become a "value-added" friend—an asset to this individual's life and business. You've demonstrated that you're in the relationship not just for what you can get out of it, but also for what you can invest on behalf of your friend. You've demonstrated reciprocity and caring. You've nourished the relationship's roots so they can become strong, deep, and broad.

When you help someone meet a goal, you instantly become a "value-added" friend.

Here's a great example of how to become a value-added friend. Coauthor Michelle Donovan created the Six Amigos Cycling Team as a way to enrich her relationships with three members of her word-of-mouth marketing team. She knew that they all enjoyed biking, and that two of their significant others would probably hop on the bikes, too, and discover some enjoyment.

She organized the Six Amigos as a way to accomplish several goals: (1) to spend more time with three people she viewed as potential members of her word-of-mouth marketing team, (2) to get to know their significant others, (3) to offer everyone an opportunity to improve their health by riding bicycles, and (4) to raise money for the American Diabetes Association's Tour de Cure.

Over the course of training for the Tour de Cure fund-raising bike ride, the team truly bonded. They became stronger friends, very supportive of each other. The Six Amigos team has since completed two Tour de Cure rides and traveled together on several bike/wine tours, including one in Canada. One member of the team said that the Six Amigos brought her and her husband together for an outdoor sport that they might never have discovered on their own.

This example clearly demonstrates how bringing value to a relationship is just as important on the personal level as on the business level. The most profitable relationships are beneficial both ways. Adding value to a relationship is also highly profitable and rewarding. How does helping someone meet a goal help you network your business? If you help someone meet a goal, he will, in turn, want to help you meet a goal: networking your business. In the Six Amigos story, Michelle helped many of her friends reach personal goals, and in the long run she developed relationships that today are helping her network her business.

Notice how Michelle took the lead in developing her relationships. You, too, need to be proactive in this regard. Many people don't openly share their goals. When asked "How can I help you?" few can answer the question. So your job, as a value-added friend, is to prepare some suggestions about how you can offer your support and help. Once you know a person's goals and challenges, approach the subject by saying something like this: "Last week you were talking about wanting to have a Web site for your business this year. I'd be happy to help you with that. Would you let me introduce you to a friend of mine who can make this become a reality?"

Here are some other tangible ways to deepen the roots of your network while becoming a value-added friend:

1. Build quality relationships. Take the time necessary to deepen the relationships between you and your referral sources. We're all driven and pressed for time, but you have to go beyond the normal business interactions with those whose support you seek. Invite them to appropriate social functions, backyard barbecues, and sporting events. Get to know these key people on your marketing team, outside the business environment, whenever possible. The stronger your friendship, the more you can all expect from each other's networking efforts.

2. Don't just show up. You might have heard the old saying "Ninety-nine percent of life is just showing up." Baloney! Just showing up is not good enough in a relationship. You must establish credibility and trust with people before you can expect them to help you in return. You need to be proactive and supportive. If you try to hurry the process, asking for something before the other person is ready, you're likely to hurt the relationship—not build your business.

3. Start by giving. Let your mantra be not "What's in it for me?" but "What can I do for you?" This is perhaps the most powerful technique for deepening and widening your networks, as well as for adding value. When building a deep network, do everything you can to bring business and contacts to your networking partners. Share information with them, and invite them to business meetings that will position them favorably with people they need to know. Get to the point where your networking partners know you always have something to give them. In short, do what it takes to earn the help you may need to ask for down the road. It's no wonder that the most effective and powerful networking entrepreneurs live by the philosophy "Givers Gain": when you help others achieve their goals, they will help you achieve your goals. Do not underestimate the power of helping other people—it is the cornerstone upon which relationships are built. If you believe, as we do, that building relationships is one of the keys to generating a continual stream of referrals, then it is an important part of the recipe for networking effectively.

The wise farmer knows that before he can expect to reap a bountiful harvest, he must invest a lot of care and energy into planting and cultivating his crop. It's hard work and long hours up front, but he knows that one day his efforts will pay him back many times over. By becoming a value-added friend, you, too, are farming. You give your time, your knowledge, and anything else of value that your referral sources need in order to succeed, knowing that one day you may draw on some of that value to help your own business.

We all know that the best time to plant an oak tree was twenty-five years ago; however, the next best time is right now! It's never too late to change your focus and develop business relationships with deep roots as well as great breadth.

> **The best time to plant an oak tree was twenty-five years ago; however, the next best time is right now!**

Week 15 Action

This week, your task is to choose one person with whom you have a strong relationship and ask the following questions. Your objective is to listen with two ears to the responses and begin to determine how you might be able to add value to this one relationship. Then set out to develop the next relationship in the same manner.

1. What would you like to accomplish with your business this year?
2. What are your challenges this year?
3. What is standing in the way of your meeting your goals?
4. How can I help you?
5. What do you need to help you be successful?

If you really listen and retain what you learn from your conversation with the person you chose for the above conversation, you will come away with some valuable tools to help make something happen for that person . . . something that will really be of value to him as he grows his business. The real winners are those who can make things happen . . . and in the following section, you will be able to practice the skills to be that kind of power-person.

☑ WEEK 16

Become a Catalyst

FOR THOSE OF US WHO DRIVE A CAR, we often take for granted a mostly silent, hidden-from-view part called a catalytic converter—at least until it breaks. What purpose does your car's catalytic converter fulfill? It removes many harmful emissions from the engine's exhaust. This is accomplished through a combination of heat and a precious-metal catalyst that causes those harmful emissions to either oxidize or be reduced to environmentally safe levels. If the engine is out of tune and not calibrated properly, the catalytic converter's efficiency can become greatly diminished—potentially leading to the converter's failure. At that point, your car is in the shop for an expensive repair.

How does a catalytic converter relate to networking your business? By definition, a catalyst is an agent that initiates a reaction. In a car, the catalyst is a precious metal. In networking, there are three kinds of people: those who wait and watch for things to happen, those who make things happen, and those who wonder what the heck happened.

In networking, there are three kinds of people: those who wait and watch for things to happen, those who make things happen, and those who wonder what the heck happened.

A catalyst is one who makes things happen. Without a catalyst, there is no spark, and not much gets done. Think of all the catalysts you know. Who is the catalyst in your home? Who is the catalyst in your office? Who is the catalyst on your favorite sports team? Who is the catalyst in your network? What would change if there were no catalysts? What would it take for you to become a catalyst for your business and your network?

Let's look at the characteristics shared by catalytic people.

Initiative. Catalytic people don't sit still—they make things happen in all aspects of their lives. These are the people who see the idea first and then take action. They are leaders by nature and take initiative simply because something needs to be done. As networkers, they stay alert for a problem that needs solving—then spring into action, calling on someone from their network to solve the problem. They operate with a "get it done now" mentality.

Intention. Catalytic people operate with intent and are goal driven. They eliminate chance by creating their own luck. They can clearly define their purpose and goals. They can envision the end and see the possibilities before others do. As networkers, catalytic people have both business and networking goals. They learn the goals of others in order to help people get where they wish to be.

Confidence. Catalytic people have confidence in themselves and in the players on their team. They also have confidence in their skills and abilities. This confidence helps to ensure that the task at hand will be accomplished with stellar results. These people have positive attitudes, seeing the glass half-full, not half-empty. Their confidence is contagious, and they tend to bring out the best in others.

Motivation. Catalytic people are not only motivated themselves, but they can also motivate others to perform at their highest potential. These people excite others to contribute, sharing their energy and excitement through their words and actions. They are in the front of the crowd, urging others to come along. They are in the back of the crowd, pushing others to keep moving forward. And they can even be seen in the middle of the crowd, rallying the masses to keep going. Catalytic people are motivated by personal and professional rewards that they can't wait to share with others. They desperately want to help others succeed.

To set your network in motion toward helping your business, make it your goal to become a catalytic person. Think of your network as a row of standing dominoes. Each domino will remain standing until you act upon the first domino. As a catalyst, you must tap the first domino to watch the chain reaction of tumbling dominoes. Your network is standing in place, waiting for you to set the pieces in motion.

Becoming a catalyst takes initiative, intention, confidence, and motivation. Your intention should be clear by now: to network your business. You took the initiative to buy this book, and we suspect that you're taking the initiative to implement the strategies in this book as well. In essence, this book is a catalytic converter for your business. All of these strategies will take some level of your initiative to catalyze the domino effect through your network. Those people in the 29% know these strategies and practice them daily.

Be confident in the abilities of your network and in the effectiveness of these strategies. Be confident that the law of reciprocity does exist. It's your job to be the team captain of your network, to motivate your players by giving of yourself. Give toward their happiness and success, and you will motivate them to give of themselves to you.

It's your job to be the team captain of your network, to motivate your players by giving of yourself.

Week 16 Action

This week, you must take the actions necessary to become a catalytic person: you must tap the first domino. Who is the first domino? Who in your network is a value-added friend? Whom do you most trust and find most credible? Reach out to that person this week, and make him aware of your intention. Then ask him for his help in networking your business.

☑ WEEK 17

Find an Accountability Partner

WHY DO PEOPLE HIRE A FITNESS TRAINER? Why do they hire a business coach? The answer, for the most part, is accountability. We tend to perform better if we are being held accountable to someone else, particularly if it is someone we respect, like a mentor or a study partner. Being held accountable for our actions, performance, and commitments tends to heighten our awareness of what we have promised to do.

> **Being held accountable for our actions, performance, and commitments tends to heighten our awareness of what we have promised to do.**

So it is with networking your business: accountability is important. As you progress through this book, you are identifying plenty of strategies that you're eager to try out. You're making a commitment to yourself to begin networking your business. You're promising yourself to get out of your cave and attend productive networking functions. You are even taking the step of putting these weekly tasks into your PDA or Outlook. But let's face it: as Nationwide Insurance proclaims in its advertising, "Life comes at you fast!" Not only that, it sends surprises your way when you least expect them. When life gets in the way, promises to ourselves get forgotten or pushed to the back burner. How many times have you told yourself in the morning that today is the day you will start to work out? As the day progressed, guess what happened? Life got in the way. Instead of getting to work out, you got worked over by life's unexpected twists.

Now, think of it this way. If you had a fitness trainer waiting for you at 6:30 p.m., would you be more committed to being there on time for your workout? Probably—because accountability kicks in (not to mention the trainer's billable time). No one likes to knowingly disappoint someone else, and no one likes to waste her time or have her time wasted by someone else. The same holds true for a business coach. No matter what happens in the week, if you have an appointment with your coach, you will find a way to complete the assignments before your meeting. The urge to comply compels us to perform at a higher level.

So why not find an accountability partner for networking your business? That way, every time you commit to a strategy in this book, your accountability partner can keep you to the task. Imagine if you and your word-of-mouth marketing team were all reading this book. Each week, perhaps by phone, you would meet to identify the strategy for the week and make the commitment to help each other meet that task. You could create a system to motivate and keep track of everyone's compliance and diligence. Perhaps the team leader—you—would e-mail everyone midweek for a brief report on the activity. Because you had someone looking over your shoulder, waiting to hear of your progress, you would be more inclined to focus on the task at hand. You certainly wouldn't risk being the only one to report nothing back the following week. Would you?

Week 17 Action

Your task this week is to identify an accountability partner. We recommend that you shy away from your friends. Friends often have trouble holding friends accountable. Picture who comes to mind when you ask yourself the following questions. Once you identify someone, call her, and begin a conversation about this book. Explain that you need her help as an accountability partner.

Questions for Finding the Right Accountability Partner

1. Who do I highly respect as a business colleague?
2. Who would not be afraid to push me and keep me focused?
3. Who would I never think of disappointing?
4. Who is also interested in networking her business so that we can be accountability partners for each other?
5. Who knows me—and my tendency to procrastinate?
6. Who will follow through on this commitment to me?
7. Who has the time to help me?

Accountability partners are particularly valuable in any formal networks you belong to. But there's a paradox: One of the strengths of any formal network is that the members of the network become friends. And—one of the weaknesses of any formal network is that the members become friends. Friends don't like to hold friends accountable—yet accountability is key in any successful referral network.

Good networking groups are not friendship organizations. They are referral networks. Granted, friendships must develop in order to make formal referral networks work. However, those very same friendships can get in the way of maintaining accountability in a group.

Why accept mediocrity when excellence is an option? Accountability in the context of a strong referral network can create excellence within that network. Fostering friendships while insisting on accountability requires a balancing act that rests on the fulcrum of a Givers Gain philosophy. We must both develop friendships and expect accountability—an accountability that is applied in a way that shows we care about people and their success.

Call it tough love.

☑ WEEK 18

Volunteer and Become Visible

ONE OF THE FIRST STEPS toward networking your business is to become more visible in the community. Remember that people need to know you, like you, and trust you in order to refer you. This strategy will focus on the "know you" part. As people get to know you, they will learn to like and trust you—at least, we hope so, because people don't care how much you know until they know how much you care.

> **People don't care how much you know until they know how much you care.**

Volunteering can position you to meet key people in your community. It connects you with people who share your passion. It gives you opportunities to demonstrate your talents, skills, and integrity, as well as your ability to follow up and do what you say you are going to do. It capitalizes on your strengths, both professionally and personally. It instantly expands the depth and breadth of your network. And it does all of this outside the business arena, so people who are getting to know you will not be experiencing you in the "customer" mind-set. You will not be selling to them. Rather, you will be giving to them.

People who volunteer demonstrate their commitment to a cause without concern for personal gain. Thus, you should be volunteering with organizations or causes for which you hold genuine interest or concern. If administrators or other volunteers perceive that you are in it primarily for your own gain, your visibility will work against you, and you will undermine your own goals.

Volunteering is not a recreational activity; it's a serious commitment to help fulfill a need. To find an organization or cause that aligns with your interests, you need to approach volunteerism with a healthy level of thought and strategy. Where would you like to invest some of your scarce free time? What would give you joy and satisfaction? What goal would your volunteering help you meet? You need to consider all these issues carefully before dedicating your valuable time.

Week 18 Action

Your task this week is to complete the following worksheet, which will help you identify your interests and passions as well as narrow and focus your volunteer options. Identifying a volunteer opportunity that's appropriate for you may take some time, so be patient, and begin the process this week.

WORKSHEET: A NINE-QUESTION SELF-ANALYSIS OF VOLUNTEER OPTIONS

1. What do you enjoy doing for yourself in your spare time?
2. What hobbies do you enjoy?
3. What sports do you know well enough to teach?
4. What brings you joy and satisfaction?
5. What social, political, or health issue are you passionate about because it relates to you, your family, or your friends?
6. Based on the answers to the first five questions, what are three organizations that you can identify that appeal to you? (Examples: youth leagues, libraries, clubs, activist groups, church groups, homeless shelters) Choose the one that most appeals to you, and research the group online and in the community.
7. Now that you've researched this group, will it give you an opportunity to meet one of your professional or personal goals? If so, visit the group to "try it on."
8. Now that you've visited this group, do you still want to make a final commitment of your time?
9. Are other group members satisfied with the organization? (To learn this, identify three members of the group to interview in order to assess their satisfaction with the organization. Consider choosing a new member, a 2–3-year member, and a seasoned 5–6-year member to interview.)

Once you've done the research required to satisfactorily answer these nine questions, join a group, and begin to volunteer for visibility's sake. Look for leadership roles that will demonstrate your strengths, talents, and skills. In other words, volunteer and become visible.

☑ WEEK 19

Send a Thank-You Card

REMEMBER, THIS SECTION is entitled "Go the Extra Mile." A simple thank-you card may not sound like going the extra mile. To many people, however, it truly is. The old-fashioned, personalized, handwritten thank-you card has been largely replaced by e-mail. When was the last time you received a traditional, handwritten thank-you card? What was your reaction? Was it "Wow, how nice that she actually took the time to write this to me"? Or was it "Gee, I can't believe she wrote this to me when she could have just e-mailed me and saved the postage. She must have a lot of time on her hands"? If you're typical, you appreciated the sender's time and effort.

In general, our society seems to be quickly moving away from the handwritten word. When you think about it, it's surprising that the holiday card industry is still holding on to its market share. But then again, more and more people order their holiday cards with their names imprinted so they don't have to sign each one. For most written communication, we simplify our lives by turning to the computer, but in doing so we make our personal messages feel somehow less personal. For that reason, a handwritten card of thanks now carries even more cordiality than when it was the norm.

A typical thank-you note might consist of three sentences. (Honestly, how long does it take to write three sentences?) Hand-address the envelope, add a postage stamp (you don't even have to lick it anymore), and off it goes to make its small but significant personal impact on one special human being. It's the next best thing to being there, and it may take you all of two minutes from start to finish. Most people enjoy receiving the handwritten card, but few actually do it themselves for other people. On the other hand, people who write thank-you cards tend to receive more of them.

You might ask, "Who has two spare minutes to write a thank-you card?" You do, if you think about it. You're sitting in your car with your kids, waiting for the school bus. You're riding the train to work. You're eating lunch alone. You're waiting forever in the doctor's office. You're sitting in a ten-mile-long traffic jam. Add those up, and we'll bet it comes to a lot more than two minutes.

Grab hold of a few of these time fragments, and use them to strengthen a networking relationship with a personal touch. Every time you make a personal connection, you are networking. Remember from the Week 7 Strategy that expressing gratitude was one of the Top Ten Traits of a Master Networker. The added exposure that makes you top-of-mind for someone will move your business forward every time.

Now, you might be asking, "When do you send a thank-you card?" Don't make it complicated. When someone goes the extra mile for you, send him a card. People we know send cards for such things as giving a referral, making an in-person introduction, helping with an event, or solving a problem.

When someone goes the extra mile for you, send him a card.

But when you send that thank-you card, remember: never, ever include your business card! (Read that sentence again, because it is very important.) There is honestly no need to send your business card to someone you are thanking. The thank-you card should be all about your gratitude, and never about pushing your business card on someone who has not asked for it. The minute you include your business card, it becomes all about YOU and not the other person. Save your business cards. Save face. And save a few trees, as well!

> **When you send that thank-you card, remember: never, ever include your business card!**

Week 19 Action

Your task this week is to first go out and purchase a set of thank-you cards that reflect who you are or what your business is. If you love gardening, find a set with a gardening theme. If your business is real estate, choose cards with a home theme. Many of these themed cards can also be found at www.SendOutCards.com, where you can design a personalized card online for any occasion, which will be mailed in an envelope, with a stamp, to the person named. If you like your technology with a personal flavor, SendOutCards.com lets you include your own handwriting, photos, and personal sentiment.

To make it even more personal, consider making your own cards, or even designing your cards with a personal caricature. Next, sit down and make a list of those who have gone the extra mile for you this past month. Finally, store some blank cards and stamps in your car and in your briefcase. That way, when you do find those two minutes of underutilized time, you'll have a card ready to write on and drop into the next mailbox you see.

☑ WEEK 20

Follow Up TODAY

THIS IS A GOOD TIME to go back and review the Week 7 Strategy. As you do, note that according to the survey of more than two thousand businesspeople, "follows up on referrals" was ranked as the single most important trait of a master networker. We believe that follow-up is the lifeblood of effective networking.

People who don't know you will judge you harshly if you don't deliver on what's expected of you. They may even test you before deciding on whether they want to get to know you better. This sizing up starts with determining whether you can make commitments and follow through on them. When your number-one objective is to cultivate strong relationships with other business professionals and build your social capital, you have to come out of the starting gate without a stumble—and this means demonstrating your commitment by following up on every promise, every contact, and every opportunity to help your networking partner, over and above what is expected of you.

Think about your own experiences, the way you form your judgments of other people and businesses. What about that time your furnace broke down and you needed repairs right away? You probably called three HVAC companies (not mentioning any names) before one finally called you back within hours. Obviously, the others, who never returned your call, will never get your business—or that of anyone you know, for that matter. They lacked follow-up, which is extremely important in building credibility and trust.

Your ability to follow up on what you say you are going to do—when you say you're going to do it—is critical toward building credibility and ultimately networking your business. Do you conduct business with anyone who doesn't do what he says he's going to do? That's exactly the point. As educated consumers, we have high expectations for service, quality, and cost. We demand to have our expectations met or surpassed. Therefore, knowing that today's consumer is so critical and demanding, we know that we must perform at our best 24/7. That includes following up on your promises. If you expect to get into the 29% as an effective networker, following up is not an option but a life-or-death requirement.

Good follow-up is not just doing what is required or what you've promised to do. It also involves going beyond what is expected. Let's say you're building a relationship with a person you've met whose profession makes her a good potential networking partner because you share a preferred client type. You've made a couple of appointments over the past several weeks, and you've followed up on solving a technical problem in her office by referring her to your favorite computer troubleshooter. Now you get news of an event that might help her professionally in another way, an event you suspect she may not have heard of. You e-mail her the Web site containing the information. In doing so, you've followed up on a conversation you had regarding her professional methods—but it's not something she expected you to do. That's why this strategy is in this section . . . that's going the extra mile. That's the kind of follow-up that not only solidifies but strengthens and extends your networking relationship. You've helped her out, and at the same time you've enhanced your reputation as the "go-to guy."

The key to good follow-up is a system for keeping track of your networking partners, your meetings and appointments with them, and their professional needs and personal interests. With this information ready at hand and easy to access, you can keep track every day of ways to enhance your value to them. It's also important to follow up in a timely manner. If you see an event or an opportunity that can be of help to someone you know, act on it immediately. Whether the affair occurs tomorrow or six months from now, pass the information along today. If you wait, you leave your colleague or contact fewer options, or you may even get busy and forget to mention it. There are few opportunities more worthless than the one that happened yesterday.

It's also important to follow up each contact at regular intervals to keep the relationship fresh in your contact's mind. If no other events or occasions come along that make it easy to network naturally, such as a business opportunity, a referral, a conference, a trade show, or some other networking event, we recommend reconnecting with your contact at three-month intervals for at least the first year. This practice keeps the impetus alive to flex the networking muscles and keep them toned up. We all get busy and distracted, but having a schedule laid out for following up at regular intervals keeps us from letting routine networking activities slip to a lower priority. Besides, it may jog your memory or that of your networking partner concerning an important event. And sometimes it's important just to call and say hello.

Week 20 Action

What's the most effective system for following up and staying in touch with your contacts? The answer is simple, and surprising: it's the one you actually use! The key is to have some kind of system for following up, and to use it. If you have a great system and don't use it, you might as well have no system at all. The following system is a simple check-off sheet that you can use to keep track of your contacts and meetings.

Your task this week is to focus on the number-one trait of master networkers and complete the Networking Follow-Up Report Card to help you follow up on all the contacts that you met last week. Duplicate this report for each week in a year, and use it to help you become more efficient with your follow-up efforts. It can also be used to help identify when it is time to reconnect with someone again. You may be inspired to create this kind of document for yourself as an Excel spreadsheet. Regardless of what you choose, select a system and begin using it this week.

NETWORKING FOLLOW-UP REPORT CARD						
Contact Name	When/Where You First Met	Follow-Up Necessary	Follow-Up Completed	3-month Follow-Up	6-month Follow-Up	9-month Follow-Up

SECTION FOUR
GET VALUE FOR YOUR TIME

HAVE YOU EVER TRIED to get back an hour you spent on something that didn't turn out well? It's not possible. Oh, you can sometimes get back the money you spent on whatever you did during that hour—but you can't recover the hour. There's no Board of Misspent Time to which you can appeal, no coupon you can send in for a free replacement hour. It's just gone. Poof!

Since you know you can't retrieve an hour, much less a day, of precious time, you obviously want to spend it as wisely and effectively as you can. In short, you want—to put it in rather calculating terms—maximum return on your investment of time. So, if you spent your time networking, you would want to get a high return on your networking investment, right?

You've come to the right place. Section Four is especially packed with strategies to ensure that you get the most for the time you invest in your networking. Weekly Strategies 21–28 suggest several ways to make networking top-of-mind in your daily activities.

The Week 21 Strategy ("Be 'ON' 24/7") emphasizes the need for you to be on the top of your networking game all the time, twenty-four hours a day, seven days a week. Networking opportunities present themselves in the most unsuspecting places and times. If you snooze, you just might lose.

Week 22's Strategy ("Learn to Play Golf or Something") challenges you to a game of golf—or some other activity that aligns with your interests and skills. A lot of business that happens on the golf course could just as easily happen on the badminton court, on the soccer field, or across the pool table!

Our Week 23 Strategy ("Have Purposeful Meal Meetings") shows you how to get more value out of your meal meetings. If you're going to meet and eat, you may as well get more out of the experience than calories. Make this activity pull its weight as an opportunity for business networking.

The Week 24 Strategy ("Make First Impressions Count") reminds us of the importance of getting off to a good start. Learn to take a closer look at your appearance and your body language. Are they helping you start good conversations—or ending them before you can even say a word?

The Week 25 Strategy ("Seek Out a Referral Networking Group") and the Week 26 Strategy ("Join a Chamber of Commerce") both build upon Week 12's Strategy ("Stop Being a Cave Dweller"). If you're going to venture out of your cave, we recommend that you seek out a referral networking group and a chamber of commerce to help network your business.

The Week 27 Strategy ("Sponsor Select Events") and the Week 28 Strategy ("Host a Purposeful Event") focus on how you can leverage sponsorship opportunities and specific events to position your business in front of key people. Of course, you need to take the initiative to make it happen.

So, now that you are out of your cave, we want you to stay out! Let's work together on these strategies so you can strengthen your network, get more return on your networking investment, and increase your visibility within the community.

☑ WEEK 21

Be "ON" 24/7

DO YOU HAVE A BROADBAND INTERNET CONNECTION at your home or office? Whether it's DSL or cable, you've probably heard your Internet service provider brag that you have an "always on" connection. No more waiting—like in the "old days" of the 1990s—while your modem dials a phone number to connect your computer with AOL, or (we're dating ourselves, here) CompuServe, or even Prodigy. Broadband service means the Internet is at your beck and call anytime you want to surf the Web.

As you saw in Week 7's Strategy ("Master the Top Ten Traits"), to be a master networker, you have to be like a broadband connection: always on. No snoozing—at least while other people are nearby. You never know when someone standing beside you might be connected to a huge opportunity. If you snooze, you lose access to that opportunity. Just as bad, the person standing there loses access to a great resource—you!

**To be a master networker, you have to be like
a broadband connection: always on.**

Here's the real kicker, the real "opportunity cost" of not being available to that person: she knows a bunch of other people who—if you're asleep at the networking wheel—will likewise never connect with you.

Did you ever see the film *Forrest Gump*, starring Tom Hanks? Forrest told the story of his amazing life to perfect strangers. He was like a broadband Internet connection, or a master networker: always on. Someone would innocently sit down on the bench where Forrest was waiting for a bus, and mere seconds would pass before Forrest would hold out a box and ask, in his inimitable drawl: "Would you like a chocolate?"

Just think. If you were to greet every "stranger" with the same openness and "always on" hospitality as Forrest, what networking adventures would unfold in your life? How many degrees of separation would you have from someone who showed a new move to a famous singer, carried wounded comrades to safety on a battlefield, greeted a US president, steered a shrimp boat through a hurricane, or simply guided a son onto a school bus every morning?

Sure, Forrest Gump was just a fictional character. But that's all you are to a stranger—a fictional character—until you open your mouth and talk. Then you're neither a stranger nor fictional—you're a real person, and a new friend.

Think of the many opportunities that come your way to talk to people in a variety of settings. How many opportunities do you typically let pass by in any given day? Now think of six degrees of separation, and imagine the people you let pass by. Which ones might have been connected to some of your preferred clients through their network? Imagine the possibilities. They're staggering!

Although we advocate being always on, and we say that networking is a lifestyle to be incorporated into everything you do, we also believe that you must network in a manner that "honors the event." By this we mean that you will network differently in some situations than in others. For example, networking at a chamber mixer is one thing, but networking at a church social is something completely different.

First, we must understand the true meaning of "networking." Networking is meant to be a proactive relationship development tool. We believe that networking is part of the process of developing your social capital. What is "social capital"? Social capital is the accumulation of resources developed through personal and professional networks. These resources include ideas, knowledge, information, opportunities, contacts, and, of course, referrals. What should the business owner keep in mind when thinking about building social capital?

Social capital is built by design, not by chance. According to Wayne Baker, author of *Achieving Success Through Social Capital*, "Studies show that lucky people increase their chances of being in the right place at the right time by building a 'spider web structure' of relationships that [catch] . . . information."[1] Furthermore, according to Baker, "success is social . . . All the ingredients of success that we customarily think of as individual—natural talent, intelligence, education, effort, and luck—are . . . intertwined with networks."[2]

Thus, networking offers a key process for acquiring social capital. Successful networking is all about proactively building and maintaining solid professional relationships. The trouble is that we don't live on *Little House on the Prairie* life anymore, and we don't have the natural community-like business relationships of that simpler era. Many business owners hardly know their own neighbors, let alone most of the other businesspeople in town. More than ever, networking is critical to an individual's success in business.

Building your social capital hinges on the development of meaningful relationships with other people. Since we should always be working on building these meaningful relationships, we should always be networking. This doesn't mean, however, that we should always be trying to sell something to someone. Herein lies the common misinterpretation of the meaning of "networking." Although some people think networking means to be constantly selling your products or services, that approach rarely facilitates the development of meaningful relationships.

Rather than constantly direct selling, the best way to build meaningful relationships is to help someone whenever possible. A good networker has two ears and one mouth and uses them proportionately. Hence, if you understand networking to be the process one uses to develop relationships and build one's social capital, then it makes sense that you should network everywhere—including the church social. The key is that you must, as we put it, honor the event.

> **Rather than constantly direct selling, the best way to build meaningful relationships is to help someone whenever possible.**

To truly honor the event, you need to network appropriately. That means in both cases—a chamber meeting and a community social event—you should make contacts, put people together, help others, and build relationships. Notice that we did not mention anything about direct selling of your business. Instead, you should simply focus on putting people together and helping others.

Trying to do business at a church function is inappropriate, but trying to help someone is not. Effective networking is all about building relationships by truly helping other people—and there's never a "wrong" time to help people. Let's use one of our own personal experiences as an example.

> **Effective networking is all about building relationships by truly helping other people—and there's never a "wrong" time to help people.**

At a church function last year, Ivan saw someone he wanted to meet. This person happened to attend the potluck brunch afterward. It would have been completely inappropriate in this context to walk up to the individual and say, "Hi, I've been wanting to meet you. I think we can do business." Frankly, we don't recommend that approach in any context, but selling so blatantly at a church function is wildly inappropriate.

What Ivan did instead was to start asking him questions about his business. He asked the who, what, when, where, and why questions and did a lot more listening than talking. He learned that the man was trying to put together a small foundation for his company's charitable efforts and finding it much more expensive and complex than he had expected.

Ivan asked the man if he was familiar with the California Community Foundation (CCF). He was not. Ivan explained that CCF (as well as most community foundations) helps individuals or companies set up funds that basically look and act as a "subfoundation" of the primary community foundation. His own foundation was set up that way, Ivan said, and he went on to explain how easy it was to do. Excited, the man asked Ivan if he could contact him on Monday and get the details. Ivan gave the gentleman his card and said he would be pleased to help.

A few weeks later, Ivan called the man to talk some business. Do you think the man took his call? Of course he did.

As you can see, keeping your networking goals in sight at all events can lead to unexpected opportunities. You want to do that, however, without becoming a networking vulture or someone people run from when they see you coming. Honor the event, and tailor your networking strategies so that you fit in—without being tuned out.

You also have to be sincere. There are people who are so successful at networking that they can network virtually anywhere, but they are successful because they really care about making connections for others, not just for themselves. Those who network exclusively for selfish gain come across as shallow and insincere.

Those who network exclusively for selfish gain come across as shallow and insincere . . . but if you are truly living the mantra "Givers Gain," you will come across very differently—and very positively.

Make no mistake about it: networking can be done with a selfish end in mind, but if you are truly living the mantra "Givers Gain," you will come across very differently—and very positively. No one minds the opportune exchange of information that will benefit one or more people, even when that exchange takes the form of a business card at a bar mitzvah.

Begin to turn on your networking button at holiday parties, at baseball games, at neighborhood picnics, at home demonstration parties, at your kid's soccer game, and at school, club, or church meetings. All of these arenas (and many more) present plenty of opportunities for network-building discussions. Keep the law of reciprocity in mind by asking someone a question that you would like him to ask you in return, such as "What do you do for a living?" or "What do you find challenging or rewarding about your job?" By asking questions like these, you can start a conversation that leads to a discussion of problems in his business—an opportunity for you to offer support by referring him to someone in your network. If you help someone, he may in turn ask how he can help you. Then it's your job to be prepared with a response that is specific.

Ultimately, the key is to be "on" 24/7 while honoring the place and the occasion at all times. Sound like a lot of effort? That's why it's called "net-WORK." It really does take a little work to network your business—and sometimes a lot.

Week 21 Action

This week is the perfect time to review your contacts with people. How many people did you engage in conversation? Were you always "on"—or were you snoozing? Did you network appropriately by honoring each event? Take this opportunity to think of next week and review your schedule. When and where will you be around people? How many new people will you talk to each day? Theoretically, if you talk to just one new person each day of the year, you will meet 365 new people by this time next year. Conservatively, let's say that of those 365 people, you actually connect with 12 (one per month). If each of these individuals knows 250 people, you could at some point be mentioned to 3,000 people in one year. That's a pretty worthwhile investment of your networking time, right?

As a strategy, being "on" 24/7 aligns nicely with several other strategies. It helps you meet more people and diversify your network (Week 8); it gets you out of your cave (Week 12); and it helps you meet your networking goals (which you set way back in Week 1). This weekly worksheet is designed to help you organize your people-centered activities and strategize about how many people you plan to meet.

People-Centered Activities	Who did you talk to there?	How should you follow up?
Wine-tasting event	1. Merlo Shiraz—owner of store 2. Shar d'Onay—editor of paper	1. Meet at store to follow up on new products 2. Call for lunch appointment to see if I can help her find columnists

☑ WEEK 22

Learn to Play Golf or Something

ACCORDING TO POLITICAL CONSULTANT Robert Hoopes (*Capital Living*, July 2005), "business" and "golf course" have been synonymous since the invention of both. Most people agree that golf outings, because of their nonthreatening nature (at least nonthreatening for those who know how to play golf), can be good for forging relationships. We know several people who learned to play golf simply because they felt they were missing out on business that was being conducted out on the greens—and that just wasn't acceptable to them.

Not everyone likes to play golf, of course. Other activities can be used to engage with people beyond the boardroom, creating an environment that's convivial and designed to forge relationships: a bowling league, a softball team, a bird-watching society, a badminton team, a billiards group, or a book club.

Whatever activity you prefer, you can use it as a "catalyst event." Catalyst events bring people together in situations that are conducive to forming symbiotic relationships. They result in great visibility, which leads to credibility and, eventually, profitability for your company—also known as the VCP Process™ of networking.

Catalyst events bring people together in situations that are conducive to forming symbiotic relationships.

How do you capitalize on the potential of your catalyst events to generate referrals for you? By inviting the right people to these events. Let's go back to that golf game as an example. You could coordinate a golf foursome with several of your business contacts—people you know who would be able to cross-refer one another, such as your CPA, your financial advisor, and your real estate investment advisor. One or more of these individuals may have been trying for months to secure a meeting with one of the others, but a golf game could be just the right catalyst to bring them together.

As these golfers develop a deeper relationship with one another, they will remember that you brought them together—and they will do what they can to make sure you are getting what you need in return. (We love the dynamic that's created when you help others get what they need; they always seem to find a way to see that you get what you need as well.)

There are, however, more creative catalyst events than the "old faithful" golf game for creating strategic alliances. For example, we know of one Salvation Army executive director who had a lot of BNI members on his board. These BNI members (being great networkers, of course) wanted to be able to serve the community and, at the same time, develop relationships with others on the board that would result in referrals for their businesses.

One of these members was a financial advisor. He had been trying to get an appointment outside the meetings with one of three millionaires who served with him on the board. Having failed by other means to secure this meeting, he changed tactics and came up with the idea of taking the entire board on a deep-sea fishing trip to help foster relationships. The charter boat used for the trip was part of the co-op advertising for the financial advisor.

The Salvation Army executive director helpfully asked the three wealthy board members if they were interested in the deep-sea fishing trip. He told them he would ask the financial advisor if they could come. This got their attention. They wouldn't take an appointment from this guy, but they were willing to do a social event of this type with him. They were all so excited about the fishing trip that one of the three who couldn't make it on the chosen date asked whether there would be another one later!

Catalyst events of this sort need to be held regularly, and repeated, if possible. Those who are invited will feel excited and appreciative, whether they can fit it into their schedules or not; others will hear about it through the grapevine and ask to be invited to the next one.

An associate recently shared a variation on this concept with us. He told us about a businessman friend of his who organized a fly-fishing trip. The trip was rather exclusive, as it was restricted to people investing $1 million or more in assets with him! The businessman and one of his guests went to the local sporting goods store to rent fly-fishing equipment. When the store manager heard who was going, he ended up giving them the equipment and a guide at no charge, just to get the exposure. The businessman then went to the local Hummer dealer—who gave them some Hummers to use if he could come with them on the trip and meet these heavy hitters.

Catalyst events must have an element of exclusivity in order to work. The people attending are investing in their social capital, too. Events at private clubs that most people can't get into, or playing golf on courses that most people can't get onto, work well. Moreover, the person hosting the event (you) must be passionate about that activity. So, if you don't like opera, don't plan a catalyst event around the opening night of *Les Miserables!*

**Catalyst events must have an element
of exclusivity in order to work.**

Week 22 Action

This week, think about your interests and what you can gain from becoming involved with a group of people who share your avocations or recreational passions. What do you really enjoy doing? What have you wanted to learn how to do? Where will you find people who share your interests? Organize an event with three or four people; start small and build it over time.

☑ WEEK 23

Have Purposeful Meal Meetings

WHAT IS A PURPOSEFUL MEAL MEETING? First, let's clarify what it isn't. It's not a way to escape work. It's not a time to have three martinis. It's not a romantic date. And it's not about critiquing new restaurants or reviewing fine wines for your local newspaper.

Oh, all those things can be great fun, no argument there. It's just that none of them are focused on (or maybe even conducive to) productive networking. From our perspective, a purposeful meal meeting is nothing more than a meeting that includes a meal and a specific, meaningful purpose. And our purpose, right at the moment, happens to be networking.

The networking purpose for this meal meeting might be to further develop the relationship, to help a colleague solve a problem, to learn how to refer someone in your network, to introduce your colleague to someone significant, or to teach someone how to talk about your business to his own network members. These meetings are strategic and results oriented. They provide high value for your invested time.

For this strategy, let's begin by considering the average work-week of five days. There are three main meals that could be eaten per day. Barring the usual hindrances to daily scheduling, this gives you fifteen opportunities each week to have a purposeful meal meeting. That's 780 opportunities in a year.

Now, dining with 780 people could not only put a hole in your pocket, but it could tear a hole in some of your personal relationships as well! Let's be realistic. Imagine what your significant other would begin to think if, for every meal, you were out with a different person. We certainly don't want to cause any family feuds or keep you away from home so much that your children or pets no longer recognize you. So, even if you conservatively say that half of those meals might be spent with your family, you still have 390 opportunities for purposeful meal meetings. And if you execute Week 11's Strategy ("Talk to Your Family"), you could actually find a number somewhere in between.

Whatever number proves right for you, the point is to realize the potential that exists for a substantial amount of networking over meals. No one capitalizes on this concept better than Keith Ferrazzi in his book *Never Eat Alone:* "I'm constantly looking to include others in whatever I'm doing. It's good for them, good for me, and good for everyone to broaden their circle of friends."[1]

This level of networking increases his productivity and helps him connect people from different parts of his community. Ferrazzi believes that his strongest links have been forged at the table. He has learned how powerful the art of throwing a dinner party can be in creating memories and strengthening relationships. Something magical and companionable happens when friends break bread together. Ferrazzi is quick to mention, however, that if we continue to have dinner parties with the same people, our circle will never grow. His solution is to identify and invite "anchor tenants" to your party.[2] These are people who are related to your core group but who know different people, have experienced different things, and thus have much to share. They tend to be the people who have had a positive influence on your friends' lives. It's akin to inviting the

CEO to the manager's table, says Ferrazzi.[3] Soon, other executives will want to be there, too.

Ivan had the opportunity to experience one of Keith's networking parties firsthand. The anchor guest that night was legendary author Gore Vidal. Providing the entertainment was America's oldest collegiate a cappella group, the Whiffenpoofs of Yale.

Clearly, not all of us will be able to get Gore Vidal and the Whiffenpoofs at our networking party—but we're guessing that Keith didn't have them at his first party, either. But the idea is sound, and you should try out the concept as a way of building your visibility in the community.

Keith has paid close attention to how a meal can most appropriately be leveraged for a business networking opportunity. However, the primary focus should always be on developing the relationship. Learning about each other, helping one another with problems, and giving of ourselves—that's what defines a purposeful meal meeting.

> **Learning about each other, helping one another with problems, and giving of ourselves—that's what defines a purposeful meal meeting.**

Relationships move our lives and businesses forward, closer to our goals. The Dalai Lama put it this way:

> We human beings are social beings. We come into the world as a result of others' actions. We survive here in dependence on others. Whether we like it or not, there is hardly a moment of our lives when we do not benefit from others' activities. For this reason, it is hardly surprising that most of our happiness arises in the context of our relationships with others.[4]

Organizing a dinner party is not a project for beginners. If you're just getting your feet wet socially, coordinating a lunch or breakfast meeting may be more your speed for now. The first step in coordinating lunch or breakfast is to consider the structure and purpose of your meeting. Let's take a closer look at two of the scenarios mentioned earlier: (1) introducing your colleague to someone significant, and (2) helping someone learn how to refer your business. With each example, we'll give you some guidance for structuring your meeting.

Example #1: Introduce your colleague to someone significant

When you introduce your colleague to someone significant, your goal is to raise the level of your colleague's credibility by giving her and her business a glowing testimonial. To prepare yourself for this meeting, learn the answers to these questions:

- What problems has your colleague solved for her clients?
- What problem were they experiencing before they came to her?
- What did she do to address the problem?
- What have been the results for the client?
- Why is she a good person for this individual to meet today?

> **When you introduce your colleague to someone significant, your goal is to raise the level of your colleague's credibility.**

If you can't answer these questions, then you need to spend more time with your colleague to better understand what she does. Let's say your colleague is a financial advisor. Based on the answers to these questions, you might say something like this:

"Kathy, thank you for taking the time to have lunch with us today. I wanted us to meet so I could introduce you in person to Sophie Lewis. Sophie is the financial advisor I mentioned to you. What I really like about Sophie is that she takes the time to listen to her clients in order to provide them with the service they truly need. It's not about selling you products. Let me give you an example. Recently, she worked with a couple in their early fifties. They came to her because they needed help balancing their plans for retirement with their current activities. She organized their savings and investments to provide them with the peace of mind that they are indeed on track for a secure retirement. The exciting thing is that this year they were able to take a long-anticipated trip to Australia without worrying that it would impact their retirement plans. They've begun to live fuller lives since they know that Sophie is there to help keep them on track. She has become their trusted advisor. You seemed to have similar concerns, so I wanted you to meet Sophie in person."

This strategy of a verbal, third-person testimonial will instantly build Sophie's credibility with Kathy. Usually, it will open up a richer conversation between them. The common link in this example is you, since you have the relationship with Sophie as your colleague and with Kathy as someone in your network who needs help. This is a win-win-win opportunity, and certainly a purposeful meeting.

Example #2: Help a close colleague learn how to refer your business

In this example, you drive the outcome of the meeting. The purpose is for someone to become more informed on how to find appropriate business for you. Your relationship is already strong, and you both have expressed an interest in wanting to help grow each other's business. To prepare for this meeting, answer the following questions with respect to one element of your business.

- What is the profile of your preferred client?
- What problems is he experiencing that demonstrate that he needs your help?
- What is he complaining about?
- What problems can he look for to indicate that someone else needs you?
- What can he say to overcome their objections?
- Who is a good referral for you?
- Who is not a good referral for you?

The person you are meeting would probably find it helpful if you provided the answers to these questions in writing. It might even be a good idea to create a handout for this meeting. At the same time, you'll be modeling what kind of information this person can provide you about his business so you can find referrals for him as well. The purpose of this meeting should be to help grow each other's business. Using this strategy will result in much stronger relationships, triwin opportunities, and increased business for you and your colleague.

Week 23 Action

If you haven't included purposeful meals among your networking goals, now's the time to determine how many you'll have each week. Open your calendar or PDA and, first, highlight all the days and times that you could utilize for purposeful meal meetings. Then proceed to your task this week: arrange three purposeful meetings. Once you have your meeting structure in order, the next step is to call three people in your network and make purposeful meal appointments this week. Make sure the other person knows the purpose of your meeting in advance. For example, tell him that you want to introduce him to someone or that you want to find out more about his business and how best to refer him to your network.

☑ WEEK 24

Make First Impressions Count

YOU PROBABLY HEARD THIS PHRASE a time or two when you were growing up: "You have only one chance to make a good first impression." The wise person who first told you this was on to something. It's the same in networking—you get exactly one chance to make that all-important first impression. People who are meeting you for the first time are judging you, whether you want them to or not.

> **You get exactly one chance to make that all-important first impression.**

How many seconds do you think most people spend sizing you up during a first meeting? Seven. That's right, in seven short seconds, you are being predefined, prejudged, and precategorized as deserving more time—or not.

It's quite scary to think that someone might choose not to relate to you based on seven seconds of interaction, isn't it? Unfortunately, it's true. (And, for better or worse, we do the same thing to other people.)

How does this seven-second window of opportunity apply to networking? As we said earlier, networking is a contact sport.

Every time you connect with someone new while networking, the seven-second clock begins its countdown. The individual begins to evaluate you based on your appearance, body language, word choice, and overall professionalism—combining them all in the blink of an eye to form her perception of you. Unfortunately, this perception, however superficial it might be, almost instantly becomes her reality.

Networking is a contact sport.

Faced with that reality—and recognizing that you need to make any amount of time you dedicate to networking as effective as possible—you must create a powerful, positive first impression. How do you do that?

Let's start with appearance. Imagine you're a fitness trainer attending a business networking event. Now, you might think that, for promotional purposes, the way you look at this networking function should be pretty much the way you look at the gym— sweatpants, sneakers, T-shirt. Maybe you have strong opinions about this. But you should ignore your opinions, because the opinions that matter are the opinions of those you're there to meet. Yes, to some degree, "dressing the part" is a valid tactic, but in this case—in our strong opinion—it would be a mistake. At the business networking function, you're representing yourself primarily as a professional business owner. You'll make a more powerful statement, especially if your preferred clients are business professionals, by wearing casual khaki slacks, a button-down shirt with your business logo (no tie needed), and dress shoes.

Next, let's look at body language. It can be the silent killer of conversations. Before you even speak your first word to a person, you've already said a lot—with your body language.

Body language . . . can be the silent killer of conversations.

Here's a good experiment to implement, sooner rather than later. The next time you're out networking, take along a trusted friend and have him observe your body language. Here are several things you can ask him to focus on regarding your performance at this event:

- Eye contact. Are you making good eye contact throughout the conversation? Or are you looking behind the person to see who else is at the event?

- Arm movement. What are your arms doing? Are they folded ("I'm bored") or tucked behind your back ("I'm interested")?

- Positioning. Are you standing in a manner that is open and welcoming, or blocking people out of your conversation? Are you leaning on something, as if bored or tired? Are you unable to shake hands because you're juggling a plateful of food?

- Facial expressions. Are you smiling, or holding back a yawn? Are you showing interest? What does your face say?

Take time to discuss your friend's observations and reactions. Listen to the feedback, become more aware, and make adjustments accordingly. Our body language is primarily subconscious—we're usually not aware of it, or of the hidden messages it sends. That's why we need the help of someone we trust to give us honest feedback.

We've already mentioned that people check you out visually within the first seven seconds of meeting you. But that's just one of the five (or six) senses they can use. What are they listening to, and how does it impact their first impression? Many people at a networking event are there with one goal: to get business. That motive, however, instantly puts a networker in a selling mind-set— and along with that comes selling-focused language and motions.

Contrary to popular belief, networking events are not meant to produce referral business on the spot. Instead, they're opportunities to build relationships that lead to more referral business. This is a different mind-set—one that should control your language and actions. Within the first seven seconds of meeting someone new, ask her this question: "How can I help you and your business?" Ask her to talk about what she does. This others-oriented approach in networking produces a powerful and positive first impression. People remember you as the person who offered to help them— not as just another person who tried to sell them something. People know when they're being sold to, and they look for ways to get out of the situation. On the other hand, most people recognize and accept an outstretched hand of support.

Contrary to popular belief, networking events are not meant to produce referral business on the spot.

Always remember that people need to know you, like you, and trust you before they will refer you. Especially "trust you"; trustworthiness is one of the top ten traits of a master networker (see Week 7 Strategy). We feel confident that if the successful participants in the six degrees study were not trustworthy, they would not have been able to enlist the help of others to complete their task. So, when you're meeting people for the first time, radiate confidence, demonstrate integrity, and begin to earn their trust. This will demonstrate your overall level of professionalism and enhance your chances of being welcomed into their network. Focusing on helping the other person helps ensure that you make a positive and powerful first impression.

Week 24 Action

Your first task this week is to look in the mirror before leaving the house and ask yourself, "What message am I sending to those who are meeting me for the first time? What opinions will they have of me before I even open my mouth?"

> **Before leaving the house, ask yourself, "What message am I sending to those who are meeting me for the first time?"**

Your second task is to become more aware of your body language by getting feedback. What are you saying without speaking a word? Take someone with you to your next networking function to give you feedback on your body language.

☑ WEEK 25

Seek Out a Referral Networking Group

HOW MUCH WOULD IT BENEFIT YOU to have several dozen sales-people working on your behalf to bring you new business? That would be something, wouldn't it? Wait, it gets better. What if you didn't have to pay them a salary or commission? What if you didn't have to provide them office space or fund their retirement plans?

> **How much would it benefit you to have several dozen salespeople working on your behalf to bring you new business?**

"OK, what's the catch?" you might ask.

There is no catch. That's what referral networks can do.

"Sounds too good to be true," you say? Well, we can't blame you for being skeptical. After all—a whole sales force for almost nothing? Most business owners don't exactly stumble across such opportunities every day, and we're taught from an early age that anything that sounds too good to be true, well, turns out to be exactly that: too good to be true (as is not true).

But this is for real. You may already be on to this not-so-well-kept secret—especially if you've read any of Ivan's other books. Just in case you're new to the world of networking, though, here are three letters you'll want to remember: BNI.

This book's coauthor, Dr. Ivan Misner, founded BNI in 1985. BNI took off like a rocket as more and more businesspeople realized that joining a referral networking group was like getting a free sales force. Since then, BNI has become the world's largest business networking and referral organization, with thousands of chapters in dozens of countries on every populated continent. Organizations like this provide a structured system for generating business by referrals. BNI's purpose is to enable professionals to develop lasting relationships that lead to future business. The motto for the organization is "Givers Gain"—which tells you up front that in order to succeed at networking, you have to help others succeed. Based on an independent study by Julien Sharp, each year the organization's participants pass millions of referrals, generating billions of dollars' worth of business for its members worldwide. No other networking organization can claim such success.[1]

BNI illustrates—simply and powerfully—why you should consider joining a referral networking group. In fact, the concept for this book arose from coauthor Michelle Donovan's active involvement with educating BNI members in her region of western Pennsylvania. She has personally experienced the benefits of BNI for her business and knows of its powerful impact on many, many others. It has become her primary forum for continuing to network her business. BNI provides a means by which many of these strategies can easily be implemented with other people who have become skilled at networking their business.

Week 25 Action

Your task this week is to visit www.BNI.com to explore the opportunities provided by BNI groups near you. Search for your city, and make an appointment to visit a chapter close by. Experience a networking forum that has purpose and is results oriented. Why settle for anything less than the best, most productive business networking organization in the world?

☑ WEEK 26

Join a Chamber of Commerce

"PUT ALL YOUR EGGS IN ONE BASKET— and then watch that basket!" This is what Andrew Carnegie in 1903 advised those who wished to become successful in business. His aphorism is well remembered and often quoted, but now it serves mainly to show us how much things have changed over the course of one century. Today, a financial advisor would typically tell you never to put all your eggs into one basket, but instead spread your exposure to risk, and diversify your income.

The same principle holds true for networking your business. Diversifying where you spend your time is a sound business networking strategy. As we explained in our Week 8 Strategy ("Diversify Your Contacts"), having a diversity of contacts—that is, networking partners with many different backgrounds and occupations—gives you more access to "linchpin" contacts and their networks. A little diversity can vastly expand the reach of your network into different professions, varied geographic areas, and diverse ways of achieving goals.

**Diversifying where you spend your time is a
sound business networking strategy.**

Last week, we talked about joining a referral networking group. By way of diversifying, let's now explore another option.

First, a question: Where are you spending your networking time right now? Perhaps you aren't doing anything related to networking, and that's why you bought this book. (Good for you!) We mentioned earlier (in the Week 9 Strategy) the importance of meeting the right people; when considering the 29% Solution, it's equally true that you must network in the right places. In order to identify the right places to network, you might want to reflect back on the profile of your preferred client from the Week 3 Strategy. Who is your preferred client, and where does she spend her time? Would it be beneficial for you to be there in the presence of your preferred client? More important, in the Week 4 Strategy we talked about recruiting your word-of-mouth marketing team— people who serve your preferred client, but for a different reason than you, and who fully believe in your products and services. If you're trying to find these people, wouldn't it make sense to network wherever they are?

Let's say, for example, that you're a project manager whose preferred client is a business that's relocating. As you identify who else serves this client, you determine that a commercial interior designer would be a perfect match for your word-of-mouth marketing team. So where can you find a commercial interior designer? By answering that question, you also determine where you need to be networking. In this example, you might find your designer in a local chapter of Commercial Real Estate Women (CREW). This will increase the value of your networking and put you next to people who also serve your preferred client. Targeting your approach this way is a smart networking habit.

By the way, CREW is an example of another type of organization you should include on any "diversify your network" list:

professional associations (sometimes called "professional societies"). There is a professional association for just about every field you can imagine (and for many more that you can't!). Professional associations are simply nonprofit (usually) organizations whose sole purpose is to support the members of a particular profession—or even a narrower niche within a broader profession—with opportunities for continuing education, networking, recognition, research, credentialing, publications, and other services.

Trade associations are similar to professional associations but focus on a particular industry or type of business rather than a profession; for example, the American Society for Training and Development. Although they often provide much the same type of service mix as professional societies, trade associations tend to get more involved in lobbying, public policy, and related advocacy efforts. They sometimes fund marketing or advertising campaigns that raise awareness of an entire industry generically, which in turn supports the more focused advertising and marketing of their member companies. Trade associations, like professional associations, offer plenty of networking opportunities—often via national or statewide conferences, trade shows, and exhibitions.

Another venue to consider: your local chamber of commerce. A chamber provides a broad membership base, but usually within a defined geographic area, such as a town or a county. This kind of local membership may or may not be important to your business. Unlike a referral networking group, professional society, or trade association, a chamber does not limit the number of people who can join from any one profession or industry. The local membership may include, for example, several commercial interior designers. Membership in this chamber of commerce would thus give you an opportunity to meet more than one prospect for your word-of-mouth marketing team.

Chambers conduct social and business events where you can socialize and develop relationships. Becoming a member of a chamber of commerce provides opportunities to give back to the community and capitalize on significant member benefits; serving in the leadership raises your recognition, visibility, and credibility, as well as that of your business.

> **Becoming a member of a chamber of commerce provides opportunities to give back to the community and capitalize on significant member benefits; serving in the leadership raises your recognition, visibility, and credibility, as well as that of your business.**

A word to the wise about joining any of these kinds of organizations (OK, two words): Get involved. The key to developing relationships of value is rolling up your sleeves and participating to the max. There's no right or wrong number of hours—just a work ethic that rewards members who really pitch in or who at least have their hearts in it. Volunteer for a committee, participate in membership recruiting drives—whatever fits your interests and available time. If you show up only for the occasional event, hoping to get lucky and meet a few people who fit your preferred client profile, not only are you wasting your time and money, but you're failing to earn the goodwill of your fellow members.

We've highlighted BNI, professional and trade associations, and chambers of commerce because of the forums they provide for networking. Keep in mind, though, that belonging to too many such organizations limits your ability to develop solid relationships and can lead to burnout. You'll get the most value out of your networking by belonging to one chamber, one referral group, and one professional association, and making yourself well known in these forums by demonstrating your abilities, strengths, and skills.

> **Diversify your eggs into more than one type of networking basket.**

Week 26 Action

We started off this week's strategy by advising you (with apologies to Andrew Carnegie) to diversify your eggs into more than one type of networking basket. Your task this week is to investigate your local chamber of commerce. Find out where the office is and request membership information. Ask for the names of members you can contact. Attend an event or two to see whether the membership is a good fit for you; for a small fee, you can probably visit a chamber mixer. Take your time, do your homework, and locate a chamber that will adequately meet your needs—and the needs of your business. Pick an active chamber that knows how to hold networking events and has strong membership. Membership is not free, but it's far less expensive than traditional advertising.

☑ WEEK 27

Sponsor Select Events

SPONSORSHIPS SEEM TO HAVE BECOME a permanent part of our consumer culture. At some time you've probably watched a televised NASCAR race, golf tournament, or tennis match, or attended a football or baseball game at a big stadium in your region. You can't watch or attend one of these events without being exposed to each event's sponsors. NASCAR's vehicles are plastered with so many company logos and decals that you can barely make them all out as they zoom around the track. Big banners are always in the background at the big tournaments and games.

On a smaller scale, local communities and organizations—be they service clubs or professional groups—also depend on sponsorships to make ends meet at some of their events. Ditto for association trade shows and exhibitions. In most cases, the dollar amounts for sponsoring events of this sort are modest—ranging from a few hundred to a few thousand dollars.

How many times have you been asked to be a sponsor? How many times have you offered to sponsor a select event in order to help out someone in your network? Both situations have the potential to give you huge exposure if done well. In addition, sponsoring an event for someone on your word-of-mouth marketing team enhances the relationship, because you are helping that person meet a goal.

When you consider which people you will network with and where, you're being selective. Choose carefully, too, when you're thinking about sponsoring an event. Is it a good investment of your time and money? Whether you're being recruited or are volunteering, ask yourself these questions before deciding:

> **Choose carefully when you're thinking about sponsoring an event. Is it a good investment of your time and money?**

- What is the target market for this event?
- What kind of exposure do I get for my investment?
- Can I get this kind of exposure without this investment?
- Do I get direct access to the audience?
- Does it make sense for me to be there?
- Which business or networking goal does it help me complete?
- Are other sponsors my competitors?
- How does this enhance my credibility with the person I'm helping?
- Why wouldn't I do it?

All of these questions help you determine the value of a sponsorship opportunity. Now, imagine one day being in charge of putting on a huge event. Suddenly, someone from your network steps forward to offer you a substantial sponsorship because she heard through the grapevine that your event needed money. How would you feel about that person? You can create that same feeling toward yourself in someone else by offering that exact gift. Be selective, and offer your support in person. In effect, you are making a tidy "deposit" in your relationship bank account. This act of generosity definitely comes back to you in time, but for now it simply nurtures the relationship by helping someone in your network meet her goals.

Week 27 Action

This week, think of the people in your network. Who is planning an event—a conference, an open house, a 10K fund-raiser—that could use your financial support? To strengthen your relationship with this individual, offer as much help from your business as you can provide.

☑ WEEK 28

Host a Purposeful Event

LAST WEEK'S STRATEGY looked at the pros and cons of being an event sponsor. This week focuses on a complementary strategy: being an event host.

We're not talking about hosting a simple dinner party or backyard barbecue. To truly earn its networking stripes, your event needs to be purposeful. It needs a goal—beyond simply getting people together.

If you were interested in hosting a purposeful event, you could easily combine this week's strategy with last week's and approach specific members of your network to sponsor the event. If your relationship is strong with those members, you could ensure that the event would meet their needs as a sponsor. Theoretically, you could provide them extraordinary opportunities for visibility and credibility. Offering this to specific members of your network could certainly enhance your relationship.

To fully understand the benefit of this strategy, let's follow an example of how one purposeful event could provide several opportunities for members of your network:

A Grand Opening

Lorrie is opening a new retail store. She's planning to host an open house by special invitation only. The first thing she needs to do is review this list of questions before planning her event.

- What is the purpose of this event?
- What is my goal?
- Who will be invited?
- Who in my network would value being in contact with my clients?
- What are my expenses?
- Who in my network has been looking for ways to help me?
- How can I help someone meet one of his business goals?
- What can I offer those who sponsor my event?

Thoughtful preparation will help Lorrie choose the right people from her network to be involved with this event. If she chooses wisely, the probability that they will say yes is high.

Based on her answers to these questions, Lorrie determines that the following people would find it beneficial to be involved in her event: a financial advisor, a business insurance agent, and a printer. All of these people would welcome exposure to Lorrie's client base. Lorrie has given each of these people her time and energy toward helping their businesses grow, so all of them now have the desire to give back to her. Lorrie has determined her event's budget and knows that three thousand dollars in sponsorship money will cover the costs. She develops a list of benefits to emphasize what's in it for her prospective sponsors. In addition, for her own information, she develops a list showing how the event benefits her business.

Benefits of being a sponsor:

- Recognition in Lorrie's event brochure, on signage near the entrance, and in her opening remarks
- Her commitment to introduce each sponsor to two people from her network
- Exposure to her network of clients, whom they may never otherwise meet
- Her commitment to sponsor a future event on their behalf, if needed
- A casual opportunity to network their business

Benefits to Lorrie's business:

- Access to a captive audience
- Media exposure for her business
- Increased traffic to her retail store
- Heightened interest in her products and services
- Opportunities to collaborate with other businesses
- Opportunities to develop business relationships with colleagues

As with Lorrie's example, planning to host a purposeful event can provide you with plenty of opportunities to give back to your network, as well as opportunities for them to give back to you. However, this is not one of those strategies that can be completed in one week. An event takes careful thought, detailed preparation, and lots of time. A book by Linda H. Schumacher, *Ready, Set, Succeed: How Successful Projects Triumph over Business as Usual*, is a great reference tool for handling this type of project. Linda shares a simple, flexible road map for navigating the complexities of planning and executing a project from its inception to its conclusion.

Purposeful events don't need to be elaborate. For example, you might choose to organize a weekly happy hour each Friday to give colleagues an occasion to build relationships. You could make it more strategic by focusing on your word-of-mouth marketing team. Hosting a wine tasting every month can bring people together around a common interest. Hosting a networking event or a luncheon so your clients can meet one another positions you as someone who adds value for everyone. This approach fits well with the points we made in our Week 15 Strategy ("Be a Value-Added Friend").

Purposeful events don't need to be elaborate.

Another good way to bring together people with a common interest is a golf outing. The combination of friendly competition, food, and camaraderie makes this a powerful event. A golf outing can be used to thank clients and referral sources for their support of your business, or to strategically bring specific people together in a casual, nonthreatening environment.

The lights in your business always shine brighter when you share the spotlight with others in your network!

Week 28 Action

Your task this week is to begin the brainstorming process to determine what kind of event you could host. It might be a grand opening, a sneak preview, a holiday gathering, or maybe an elite mixer for key people in your network. Here are some questions to ask yourself: How would a given event develop and nurture relationships with specific individuals in your network? How might you collaborate, with them or others, for joint success? What value could your event bring to the members in your network? What goals would you like it to accomplish?

You can help the members of your network showcase their businesses, and network your own business in the process. The lights in your business always shine brighter when you share the spotlight with others in your network!

SECTION FIVE

CONTROL YOUR COMMUNICATION

DID YOU EVER PLAY THE CHILDHOOD GAME called "a whisper down the lane"? Perhaps you knew the game by another name, such as Broken Telephone. One player whispers a message to the person sitting next to him in line. That person then has to whisper exactly the same message to the next person, and so on down the line. The relayed message invariably gets contorted, amid snickers and perplexed giggles, before reaching the last person in the chain. The end result is often quite funny, with the final whispered message bearing little resemblance to the original. Words get lost or twisted, and more dramatically, the original meaning is often lost entirely. The longer and more complex the starting message, the less chance it has of surviving the trip.

As a game, this can be funny—but in real life, when it involves your business, it's no laughing matter. In word-of-mouth marketing, communication is critical; success rests on the delivery and impact of your message.

What do we mean by your "message"? In this context, it's the description you give of your business and your preferred client whenever you introduce yourself to someone in a one-on-one networking encounter or to a group during a presentation. It's typically a sentence or two, taking perhaps ten seconds to deliver.

If your message is too complex, lacks passion, or flies over the listener's head, it will probably not be memorable. If it's not memorable, it can't be repeated. If it can't be repeated, it won't survive the word-of-mouth "whispering chain." Worse, your message might reach its destination, containing not only mysterious words but a convoluted meaning.

For example, you thought you said, "Hi, my name is John, and I operate a business that brings first-time mothers and their newborns together with dogs to help infants and pets adjust to living safely together." Somehow, though, by the time the person introduces you at a network meeting, your message has been transformed: "Hi, everyone, I'd like to introduce you to Joe. He operates on infants who have been attacked by dogs. Let me just say, Joe, that it's wonderful you donate your time for such an important cause!"

Obviously, this is not a good scenario. Your message and your identity have been garbled. You can imagine what kind of impact this could have on your business. What immediate effect does it have on your ability to network? What does this tell you about your message and your word-of-mouth marketing team? Effective communication is absolutely necessary for a successful word-of-mouth plan to succeed.

Each weekly strategy in this section (Weekly Strategies 29–33) will focus on how to clarify your message so it can be successfully passed on to someone else. Here's an overview:

The Week 29 Strategy ("Ask Your Own Questions") shows you how to capitalize on the law of reciprocity in getting your message out through networking.

The Week 30 Strategy ("Talk About Benefits, Not Features") addresses the content of your message. Studies show that people make purchases based on benefits, not features—a factor you need to consider when framing your business's message.

The Week 31 Strategy ("Become a Profiler for Your Business") challenges you to wear the hat of a profiler when describing your business to people in your network. It's been shown that the more specific your profile, the higher the return on your networking investment.

The Week 32 Strategy ("Become a Motivational Speaker for Your Business") taps into the passionate motivational speaker hidden deep within you. The passion that drove you to where you are today should influence your marketing efforts, including your word-of-mouth plan.

The Week 33 Strategy ("Leverage Your Smallest Billboard") demonstrates how to get the most out of your smallest, cheapest billboard: your business card. Your card often plays a key role in making your first impression. Its communication power is under-utilized, overlooked, and sometimes abused.

Several of these strategies can be implemented easily. A concerted effort to modify the way you speak and represent your business will let your true passion shine. Make your message authentic and motivational, and your networking partner will "whisper it down the lane." Make it clear and concise, and it will arrive intact at the target: your preferred client.

☑ WEEK 29

Ask Your Own Questions

THROUGHOUT THIS BOOK we've talked about the law of reciprocity. In business, it's critical to understand how this ties into human nature. Most of us have been taught as children that if someone does something nice for you, you should someday return the favor. Think about how you feel when someone goes out of her way for you. You probably resolve not to forget about it, and in fact you may make a sincere effort to repay her quickly. The law of reciprocity guides our obligations and commitments to each other, because most of us don't like to feel obligated to others.

> **Most of us have been taught as children that if someone does something nice for you, you should someday return the favor. The law of reciprocity guides our obligations and commitments to each other, because most of us don't like to feel obligated to others.**

In business, that's a good thing. You can usually count on reciprocity and be assured that the time and effort you give someone will come back to you. Look at it as a "relationship bank account." Every time you do something nice for someone, you make a deposit of goodwill into your account at his bank. When you feel you've deposited a substantial amount of goodwill, it may be time to withdraw something from the account by asking for a favor.

> **You can usually count on reciprocity and be assured that the time and effort you give someone will come back to you.**

The law of reciprocity even has an impact on our conversations when we're networking. If you want someone to ask you a specific question, ask her the same question first. She'll think, "That's a great question." After she answers, she'll probably ask you the same question in return. (If she doesn't, she might be an "all about me" person—someone you want to avoid.)

> **If you want someone to ask you a specific question, ask her the same question first.**

Let's be more specific. Here are ten great questions to ask someone while networking that are then likely to be asked of you in return.

1. What do you do?
2. Who's your target market?
3. What do you like most about what you do?
4. What's new in your business?
5. What's the biggest challenge for you and your business?

6. What sets you apart from your competition?

7. Why did you start your business?

8. Where is your business located?

9. What's your most popular product?

10. How do you generate most of your business?

In his book *Endless Referrals*, our good friend Bob Burg posed what may be the single best question we've heard to ask someone about what he or she does. Bob writes that the question "must be asked smoothly and sincerely, and only after some initial rapport has been established. The question is this: 'How can I know if someone I'm talking to is a good prospect for you?'"[1]

Bob is right on the mark with this question. It separates you from the rest of the pack; it's a question that the average person doesn't ask. And it demonstrates one of the top ten traits of a master networker: helpfulness (see Week 7 Strategy).

Week 29 Action

Before attending your next networking function, think about what you want other people to ask you. To get the most out of the law of reciprocity, take the initiative and ask those questions of each person you meet. If you do, you will accomplish several things: (1) you will find out whether this person is someone you want to know better, based on his preferred client and his personality; (2) you will offer support to him instead of selling to him, which will open more doors for the conversation; and (3) you will give yourself opportunities to network your business more effectively.

This is also a good week to remember, from Week 7's Strategy, that one of the top ten traits of a master networker is good listening skills. So, though you are asking questions with the hope of having them asked to you in return, don't neglect this fabulous opportunity to gather invaluable information that you can use—both now and in the future—about the person you chose to query!

☑ WEEK 30

Talk About Benefits, Not Features

SALES TRAINING OFTEN TEACHES YOU that customers make buying decisions based on (1) their emotions ("Sell the sizzle, not the steak!") and (2) the value the product or service brings to them. Marketing specialists capitalize on customers' emotion-based buying habits. Customers choose a product or service based on its benefits, not its features. The features are simply the bare-bones facts—the elements or significant parts—of the product or service. The benefits are its value to the customer—how it will solve their problems, eliminate their pain, and make life glorious.

To understand the difference, think about a car:

Features of a Car

- V-6 engine, dual exhaust, front-wheel drive, sunroof, significant interior legroom, heated seats, heated glass

Benefits of those features

- V-6 engine—ability to pull onto the highway without hesitation (and to impress your friends)
- Dual exhausts—higher fuel efficiency and more power (and it sounds groovy and also impresses your friends)
- Front-wheel drive—more interior room because of the lack of a driveshaft tunnel
- Sunroof—the open feel of a convertible with the safety and security of a sedan
- Legroom—greater comfort while driving long distances and more room for your growing family
- Heated seats—cozy motoring on frigid days and nights; greater back comfort on long-distance trips
- Heated glass—the convenience of not having to scrape icy windows in the winter

The more perceived value a benefit offers, the higher it gets ranked in your decision to purchase. Objectively, a sunroof is not a significant feature, but if it makes you feel a bit like a race car driver, perhaps that benefit raises its value for you. Heated seats are nice too, but they might not rank high in value to people who live in a warm climate and wouldn't strongly influence their buying decision. The benefits of dual exhausts, however, might have perceived value for all buyers—better fuel efficiency, more power, and a sound like your beloved but departed '57 Chevy.

What does all this have to do with your word-of-mouth marketing message? Simply this: Most businesspeople, without thinking about it, talk in terms of features. As professional experts and salespeople, that's what they're most familiar with. They're not accustomed to looking at their products or services from a customer's perspective.

In formulating the message you want your networking partners to convey, your challenge is to put yourself in the customer's place. What are the benefits of your product or service? How will they make the customer's life or business easier, more comfortable, more satisfying, more profitable? How can you shorten and simplify your message so that others can communicate these benefits more clearly and more surely?

Week 30 Action

To zero in on the benefits of your business, your first task is to focus on your best customers. What problems were they experiencing before they came to you? What problems did you solve for them? How did you make their lives easier? The answers to these questions will begin to connect you with their motives for buying your products or services. You provided some value to them that was significant enough to cause them to spend their money. What was it?

An additional task this week is to complete the worksheet that follows, on the features and benefits of just one product or service you offer. Once you've done so, begin to include the language of your benefits in your messages to your marketing team, to prospects, and while networking. It would be a good idea to complete this worksheet eventually for each of your products or services. The Week 31 Strategy ("Become a Profiler for Your Business") will help you simplify your message and make it more specific.

WORKSHEET: FEATURES VS. BENEFITS

(Do not limit yourself to this sheet!)

Product or service: _____

FEATURE of this product or service	BENEFIT of this feature

☑ WEEK 31

Become a Profiler for Your Business

COMMUNICATION IS ALWAYS A CHALLENGE. If it were easy, there would be no need for research, books, or training programs on the subject, and there would be far fewer divorces—and wars. But communication is doubly vital in networking. Your success in marketing your business by word of mouth rests mostly on your skills as a communicator. The clearer and more concise your message, the more easily it is passed on by your marketing team.

> **Your success in marketing your business by word of mouth rests mostly on your skills as a communicator.**

Here are three common ways people miscommunicate:

1. They talk too much.
2. They use jargon.
3. They speak in generalities.

Doing any of these things is a mistake that can cause your message to be lost, misheard, or ignored. Worse, it can create misinformation or confusion, or even turn people against you, causing you greater harm than if you had not tried to communicate at all. Let's look at these communication traps one by one.

The first trap, talking too much, is one that we've all found ourselves downwind of from time to time: the overeager car salesman; Aunt Mabel gossiping on the phone; the self-absorbed running back; Charlie Brown's schoolteacher, going "blah, blah, blah." Whatever you call it—logorrhea, verbal throw-up, "I" trouble, running off at the mouth—if you're guilty of inflicting it on other people, it can doom your hopes of networking your business.

Talking too much is often a sign or result of just plain nerves. You're meeting a prospect or a contact for the first time, and you're worried that you won't have anything to say or won't have time to explain the marvels of your business. You can overcome your nervousness by recognizing when it's time to stop talking. Look for signs in the other person's body language: avoiding eye contact, stepping back, looking over his shoulder, yawning, looking at his watch.

Before you go to a mixer or other networking event, say this aloud to yourself before entering: "Tell me about your business." Repeat three times. Then walk in with this simple sentence running in the back of your mind. Once you're engaged in conversation, and after you've said a few words to introduce yourself, voice your rehearsed query (or some variation keyed to the context of your discussion) to your prospect: "That's fascinating! Tell me what a canine ophthalmologist does." The law of reciprocity (see Week 29 Strategy: Ask Your Own Questions) gives you a pretty good chance that your listener will ask you later about your own business.

The best way to avoid nervous over-talking is to simply ask a question, relax, and let the other person talk. This will let her know that you're interested in finding ways to help her; it will give you valuable information about how this person might fit into your network to your mutual benefit; and it will show that you're not a self-absorbed, compulsive schmoozer, out to grab all the business you can get. Most importantly, when the tables rotate and it's your turn to talk . . . pay attention to the non-verbal cues that it's time to stop talking.

The second trap, the jargon attack, is sprung when we talk over the listener's head. This often happens when we are so eager to tell about features that we neglect to mention benefits (see Week 30 Strategy: Talk About Benefits, Not Features). Suppose you're an IT consultant, and someone asks you about your work. If you find yourself spouting phrases like "the split GPO approach to firewall management" or "software-intelligence-enabled real-time use of unstructured data"—hey, you're in danger of putting even yourself to sleep. Unless you're talking shop with another IT consultant, it's going way over the head of your listener, who's going to simply shut down and stop listening—another victim of "jargon jaw."

Any of us can be guilty of "jargon jaw," because each of us knows our industry so well that we tend to speak its language regardless of who's listening. In a networking situation, remember that unless you are speaking to someone else in your industry, you must eliminate jargon from your vocabulary. Simplify your message so the average person can relate to what you're saying. When someone asks you, "What do you do for a living?" here's how you should respond:

- Instead of saying, "I do IT consulting and system hard drive analysis," say, "I troubleshoot and tune up computers to keep them free of problems." It's easy to relate to computers that are problem free, but terms like "IT consulting" and "hard drive analysis" are confusing to some.

- Instead of saying, "I'm a marketing consultant," say, "I help businesses become known in the community."

- Instead of saying, "I analyze telecommunications hardware and systems," say, "I save businesses money on their phone systems."

Notice that in these examples we eliminated the industry jargon and replaced it with a benefit statement. That is, we went from industry-specific, feature-related terms to less-specific, benefit-related terms.

The third trap is speaking in terms that are too general. In networking, general requests are hard for people to fulfill, because they don't bring to mind specific people or situations that the listener may know of.

Suppose you ask a realtor what kind of prospect he wants to meet, and the realtor says, "Anyone who wants to sell a home." The chances of your knowing someone who "wants to sell a home" are slim, and if you do know someone who is putting her house on the market, she's probably already dealing with a real estate agent. But if the realtor says, "Empty nesters looking to downsize," you immediately think of two or three couples whose last child has moved out. This answer is more specific, and it makes you think of home owners who may be just starting to consider moving to a smaller house.

It may seem odd to you, but the more specific you are, the wider the door opens in the listener's mind. Police profilers know the value of being specific. If a witness's description of a crime suspect is too general, the likelihood of finding that suspect is slim. In networking, the more specific your description of your preferred client, the more likely it is that someone will know him. To network your business effectively, think of yourself as a profiler. The more accurately you profile your preferred client and the more specific your message, the better your referrals will be.

Being specific also helps when you ask someone to help you. Let's say you're looking for a personal introduction to the CEO of Company X. When you ask someone in your network to introduce you, be specific: "John, could you arrange a one-hour lunch meeting for the two of us and Ruth Sinclair, the CEO of Company X? She's someone I'd really like to meet, and since you know both of us well, it would be great to have you there." This request is specific; it gives John the details he needs to successfully complete the task.

Week 31 Action, Part I

A surefire way to avoid talking too much is to practice delivering your message. Here's the most-asked question in networking: "So, what do you do for a living?" Practice your response to this question, and time yourself until you can answer it concisely and clearly in one minute. Keep in mind that the question is what you do for a living, not how you do it. Remember the questions from the Week 29 Strategy ("Ask Your Own Questions")? Your first task this week is to time a one-minute response to each of those questions.

Week 31 Action, Part II

Your second assignment will be to identify ten jargon words that you've been using in your networking. Write them down on the following worksheet, and brainstorm how you can communicate those words in layperson's terms. It might be helpful to get insight from a colleague outside your profession, since, as we mentioned, sometimes we're not aware of our own jargon, because we're too close to the subject.

WORKSHEET: ELIMINATE JARGON JAW	
Jargon words or phrases	**Saying the same thing in layperson's terms**
1.	
2.	
3.	
4.	
5.	
6.	
7.	
8.	
9.	
10.	

Week 31 Action, Part III

Your third and final task for this week is to write out a referral request before presenting it to the people in your network. Make the request specific by using the name, company, and profile of the person you want to be referred to. Create a clear image of what the people in your network should be looking for and what you want them to do on your behalf. As an experiment, show your written request to someone close to you and ask him if it is clear, concise, specific, and devoid of assumptions. Becoming an effective profiler for your business not only helps you clarify your messages, but it also helps ensure the success of your word-of-mouth marketing efforts.

☑ WEEK 32

Become a Motivational Speaker for Your Business

SO FAR, we have firmly established the need for your message to be clear, concise, and specific. Another element that's very important in networking your business by word of mouth is the delivery of your message. In fact, how you deliver your message is sometimes more important than the message itself.

Have you ever listened to a motivational speaker such as Jack Canfield, Brian Tracy, or Zig Ziglar? What were you feeling as you listened? What did the speaker do to connect with you on an emotional level? What was hidden deep within the speaker's message? The hidden element behind a motivational speaker is passion.

As you listened to that speaker, you could feel the passion flowing through the presentation's words, actions, and images. Passion penetrated your heart; passion moved you, touched you, and inspired you; passion impelled you to spread the word about this extraordinary speaker.

Think about that. Without passion, the speaker's message would have been flat, uninspiring, and certainly not motivating. Without passion, that motivational speaker would have failed. The presentation would simply have been ordinary. What does this tell you about your own message?

Now, slip into the shoes of that motivational speaker. You, your sales force, and your word-of-mouth marketing team are the motivational speakers for your business. But the message begins with you. Indeed, it begins within you. Never forget (see Week 7 Strategy) that one of the top ten traits of the master networker is enthusiasm/motivation.

It's your choice: Will the message come from your head or from your heart? When the message comes from your head, it's intellectual and unemotional; it's just facts, figures, and features. But a message from the heart is filled with emotion and passion. Which type of message would set you apart from others in your industry? Which would attract people to you as if you were a motivational speaker? If you were on the receiving end, which would you prefer? Which approach would inspire you to pass the message along to someone else?

> **It's your choice: Will the message come from your head or from your heart? When the message comes from your head, it's intellectual and unemotional; it's just facts, figures, and features. But a message from the heart is filled with emotion and passion.**

Your personal challenge in networking is to have an extraordinary message that not only captures but also highlights your unique selling proposition (USP). Your USP is what sets you apart from your competition; it's that element about you and your business that your competitors cannot claim for themselves. You can't afford to be ordinary, like your competition. You can't afford to fail. Your message needs to be filled with passion. If you are not excited about what you do, no one else is either. In word-of-mouth marketing, that could be disastrous.

Your USP is what sets you apart from your competition.

So how do you tap into your passion and tie it into your daily message about your business? How do you do what you do better than anyone else? Do you love what you do? Does your work truly make you happy? Do you love it so much that you would still do it even if you didn't get paid for it? Why? How does it fulfill you? You know you've tapped into your passion when you can answer those questions without any hesitation. The secret here is that your word-of-mouth marketing team must feel your passion and be able to re-create it on your behalf when they talk with others about your business. Like your USP, your passion is what separates you from your competition. Passionate people can infect others with their passion, further enhancing their success at finding your business and helping you with your goals.

Week 32 Action

Your task this week is to touch the inner spirit of your business and draw it to the surface. Reveal it to yourself and to your marketing team. Capitalize on the passion within your heart. Spotlight your uniqueness. Specifically, answer the following few questions, and be sure to respond to them from your heart and not your head.

1. What can you say about yourself or your business that your competition cannot say?
2. How does your work fulfill you?
3. What element of your work do you most enjoy, and why?

Leverage Your Smallest Billboard

HAD YOU DRIVEN ALONG many of America's highways back in the 1930s, '40s, and '50s, some unusual messages posted on roadside signs (one after the other) would have enlivened your trip. Here's a sample:

DINAH DOESN'T

TREAT HIM RIGHT

BUT IF

HE'D SHAVE

DINAH-MITE!

Burma-Shave

Catchy and kitschy, these little rhymes hooked Burma-Shave solidly into the American psyche and made the little billboards on which they appeared cultural icons for a generation. In an era when electric shavers were still considered luxury gadgets and nearly all men used shaving cream and razors every morning, these minibillboards gave Burma-Shave name recognition and solid profitability. Corporate conglomerates eventually gobbled the company up, but Burma-Shave's powerful branding and marketing lesson lived on.

You have the same opportunity as Burma-Shave to hook yourself into the minds of people you meet while networking. And you have very nearly the same tool with which to achieve that goal: your business card. Sure, it's a lot smaller than a roadside sign. But it's a billboard nonetheless.

An effective business card is an integral part of a good marketing plan. For its size and cost, it's probably the most powerful marketing tool you own. Take one of your cards out right now and look at it. Does your current card accurately reflect your business's personality—and your own? What kind of first impression does it make? Is it memorable? If not, it will probably get tossed into a drawer full of ancient, bent, forgotten cards that keep accumulating long after the businesses they represent have faded away. (That is, unless it gets dropped into the nearest circular file and eventually ends up in the long-lost business card landfill.)

Of course, you can't expect your business card to do all the heavy lifting by itself. It can't tell the whole story about your company. It's not a brochure or a catalog. It has limited space, so you have to choose your words and images carefully. Nevertheless, your card should present a professional image that people will remember. A business card can make or break a client's first impression of your company. In fact, this little billboard makes as much of an impression as your personal appearance. (For a refresher on the importance of first impressions, you might want to refer to the Week 24 Strategy.)

Choose a card style that's appropriate for your business, industry, and personal style. If you're a funeral director, you don't want to be caught handing out Day-Glo cards with cartoon figures on them. If you're a mechanic whose specialty is converting old VW Beetles into dune buggies, a formal, black-on-white engraved card will probably be thrown out. Start with the style that best supports the business image you wish to project. Here are five different card styles for you to consider:

Choose a card style that's appropriate for your business, industry, and personal style.

Basic cards. This is a good card style when utility is all you need. It's a no-nonsense approach that can appeal to clients and prospects who would not be impressed by fancy design features—the people who want "just the facts, ma'am." The design is simple, and the information is clear and concise. A basic card is usually printed in black ink on plain white or cream stock.

Picture cards. Having your face on your card—whether it's a photograph, a drawing, or a caricature—helps a contact remember you the next time she sees you. Images representing a product or service, or a benefit your business provides, can help you communicate your business better than dozens of words. A splash of color (rather than just black and white) is often helpful on a picture card, too.

Tactile cards. Some cards are distinguished not so much by how they look as by how they feel. They may use nonstandard materials, such as metal or wood, or have unusual shapes, edges, folds, or embossing. Tactile cards tend to be considerably more expensive than regular cards because they use nonstandard production processes, such as die cuts. But, for some businesses, this unusual card may be worth the investment.

Multipurpose cards. A card can do more than promote your name and business—it can also serve as a discount coupon, an appointment reminder, or some other function. It may also provide valuable information that the average person might need. For example, a hotel may include a map on the back of its card for any guests who are walking around the vicinity. A card of any type can be made multipurpose by adding features like these.

Outside-the-box cards. A wildly original, fanciful, or extravagant presentation can draw extra attention. Creativity knows no bounds—except the amount of money you wish to spend. Some examples are cards made of chocolate, cards fashioned into a deck of playing cards, or cards that fold out into a miniature box that holds small items. One of the most memorable we've seen is a dentist's card that includes a small compartment for dental floss to be pulled out. These are all examples of "outside-the-box" business-card thinking.

Regardless of the style you choose, the impact must remain consistent. For more detailed descriptions of the different types of business cards and their impact, take a look at the book *It's in the Cards*, by Ivan Misner, Dan Georgevich, and Candace Bailly. The authors reviewed more than two thousand business cards from ten countries. More than two hundred of the best examples appear in the book in full color.

Week 33 Action

Your first task this week is to look closely at your business card and ensure that it truly and positively represents you and your business. Though the following advice may seem obvious, failure to heed it may cost you another trip to the printer: Check for the essentials. This means your name, title, company name, address, phone number (or numbers, if you want to include your cell phone), e-mail address, and Web site. If someone wants to contact you after receiving your card, you sure as heck want him to be able to reach you immediately.

Your second task: Think about how and when to deliver your business card. How many times have you been to a networking function and had people come up to you and literally push their cards into your hand or pocket? Such behavior is business card abuse, and it warrants a phone call to the business card police. We call these people "card pushers." They come directly from the school of power networking, where they've been taught to "Sell! Sell! Sell!"—and to do so at networking events by forcing their cards on every person they meet. Their goal for each networking event is to get rid of as many cards as they can, under the illusion that simply having a card automatically makes you part of their network. They make no real effort to develop relationships. Being on the receiving end of such aggressive card mongering feels awkward; you are being directly sold to, with no consideration of your interests or needs. Does this sound like a cold call to you? It is—except for one thing. The seller is not safely out of reach at the other end of the line—he's breathing in your face and grabbing your hand.

It's a situation you'd like to avoid, right? Then make every effort not to impose it on anyone else. Don't hand out your business card unless someone asks for it.

That's right. You read correctly. We'll say it again to make the point. The best way to use your business card is not to give it out if people don't ask for it. If you practice this rule while networking, you'll be amazed at the impact you'll have on others. You'll find it refreshing, liberating, and, most important, controlled. You are now assured that people who ask for your card actually want your card. As a bonus, you save money and trees!

So, you may be asking yourself, what happens if I want to give someone my card, but she doesn't ask me? It's simple. Do you remember the law of reciprocity mentioned in the Week 29 Strategy ("Ask Your Own Questions")? First, ask her for her card. As she hands you her card, she will probably ask you for yours as well.

SECTION SIX
BECOME THE EXPERT

BECOMING THE EXPERT is a surefire way to attract people to your corner of the world. Authors and journalists are always looking for experts to quote. People in general like to be able to say they know an expert; it adds to their credibility and makes them feel more important.

Authors and journalists are always looking for experts to quote.

Achieving a reputation as an expert is not as difficult as you might think—although, as with anything worth doing, it takes time, effort, and persistence. This section spotlights four strategies you can put in motion to become known as an expert.

The Week 34 Strategy ("Give a High-Value Presentation") encourages you to go on the speaker's circuit to spread your knowledge and, thus, your perceived value.

The Week 35 Strategy ("Create an Informative Newsletter") presents the idea of creating a newsletter through which you can periodically convey valuable, useful information about your business or industry—and position yourself as the expert.

In this section, the Week 36 Strategy ("Write a Press Release") and the Week 37 Strategy ("Write Your Own Identity") will take the majority of your time. However, writing yourself into the public eye definitely positions you as the expert and increases your credibility. The long-term value is immeasurable.

☑ WEEK 34

Give a High-Value Presentation

WHEN YOU SCHEDULE AN APPOINTMENT with someone you think might be interested in what you're selling, the time you spend with him is important. Imagine having that same appointment with twenty to fifty businesspeople in your community, all at the same time! In effect, that's what you're doing when you're asked to make a presentation. Getting speaking engagements is a great short-term approach to building your business. And it fits well with your long-term process of word-of-mouth marketing, because educating your referral sources takes time.

Educating your referral sources takes time.

Let's say you manage to get yourself invited to speak to a group, and you're not sure what to talk about. Why not just cut to the chase and give a presentation to help people better understand what you do? Well, unless you're speaking to your daughter's sixth-grade class on Career Day—in which case at least one other person in the room is likely to find your remarks interesting—why would you expect a roomful of busy, time-stressed people to think that what you do is so enthralling? Are you an astronaut? Unlikely. Are you the president of a major country? Probably not. Chances are you're a businessperson or a professional.

Almost anyone can get up and ramble on about his business. Unfortunately, the only person who seems to be entertained by such a spectacle is the speaker. Maybe you've sat through presentations like that.

Don't worry. That's not the kind of presentation we're suggesting you deliver. A glorified sales pitch won't cut it. Instead, we've got two words for you: high value.

Remember what we said back in Week 30? "Talk About Benefits, Not Features"? Well, there's a similar idea at work here when you're making a presentation. If you spend your half hour talking about "what I do," you're giving your listeners the features. That's a nonstarter, an invitation for an MEGO ("My Eyes Glaze Over") response from the audience.

But if your presentation gives your audience something they can use—information that will help them in business or at home, issues and trends they need to be aware of, or even a compelling, inspiring, entertaining talk that leaves them feeling energized and motivated—that's a high-value presentation.

What, exactly, does "high-value" mean? It means you think about the people you'll be speaking to, consider their needs and interests, and craft your presentation to raise their awareness about a topic that's important to them—while subtly raising their awareness of your expertise as well. It's a classic instance of "Givers Gain" at work.

Our experience has shown that you often get new business simply from speaking to a group. When you're known for delivering high-value presentations, you get more invitations to speak. And the more you speak, the more you attract new contacts, new opportunities, new referral sources. Therefore, if you focus on providing high value in your presentations, you'll reap the rewards.

Where can you make such presentations? While you may realize the immense networking value that joining and participating in service clubs lends to your credibility in your community, what you may not think about is how much business you can generate by speaking at these various meetings. That's why we recommend that you focus first on securing speaking opportunities at service clubs and business organizations right around your own home base.

Getting on the calendars of these business and service groups isn't as hard as you might think. With a little creativity, you can put together a presentation that is informational, educational, and even entertaining for these groups. Most importantly, you can get referrals from people to help get you in front of them. The program chairs of these organizations are usually scrambling to find someone different, engaging, and interesting to come in and make presentations to the group. Your job is to help them find you.

Here is an example of a letter one man gave to specific people to make it easy for them to refer him for a speaking engagement. Notice that there is far more value being offered here than in a traditional one-hour sales pitch.

Dear Program Chair:

XYZ Consulting is a management consulting firm that works with small and midsize businesses. During the past two years, we've given a presentation entitled "Entrepreneuring in the '80s" to more than 60 service organizations such as yours. The presentation deals with managing and motivating employees. It involves participation and interaction with the audience, and leaves time for questions at the end. Here are some of the comments we've received:

"Fantastic, every service club must hear!"
—East LA Rotary

"An excellent talk by an excellent speaker."
—Irwindale Rotary

"Excellent, highly recommended, got a lot of questions."
—Hermosa Kiwanis

If you're interested in this topic, we'd be glad to visit your club to give this presentation.

Please feel free to contact us if you have any questions.

Sincerely,

President, XYZ Consulting

This letter was taken to networking meetings and given to people who wanted to refer business to this company but didn't know how. The resulting speaking engagements ended up bringing in a lot of business—including what turned out to be one of this company's largest clients.

Once you've prepared and rehearsed your high-value presentation, we recommend that you compose your own letter along these lines. Just one person who contacts you because of this letter can put you in front of many others who might be in the market for your product or service. Once you have the opportunity to make connections like these, you never know where they'll lead.

Let's look at an example of how a hardware store owner positioned himself to be a speaker at an organization's weekly meeting. You might wonder: How could a hardware store owner appeal to a program chair looking for someone to speak to a business group? Easy. Home safety is always a timely topic. Who better than a hardware store owner to fashion a presentation on home safety and give valuable tips on things to do around the house to be sure that the home environment is free from hidden and not-so-hidden dangers? Of course, the members present at that meeting may have a need to take care of some of the things the presenter brings up. Who do you think they're going to contact? Bingo! That week's speaker is just the person for the job.

The key is to go in with information and education—a high-value presentation—not a huge sales pitch. People don't like being sold to, but they do like to buy! A great presentation makes your audience want to buy what you're selling, as long as you're not hard-selling. A great presentation can also position you favorably for extended networking with the members and their contacts. This technique makes it easy for people to refer you.

> **Go in with information and education—a high-value presentation—not a huge sales pitch.**

Week 34 Action

Your task this week is to compose your own letter outlining a high-value presentation that you're qualified to give to your target market. Create ten copies of the letter, and give it to your extended network to enlist their help in referring you for presentations.

☑ WEEK 35

Create an Informative Newsletter

THINK ABOUT THE PEOPLE you consider experts. They are known for sharing their knowledge—through books, research papers, columns, articles, and newsletters. Experts write. If you wish to be seen as an expert, consider writing an informative newsletter.

Of course, you don't just sit down and crank out a good newsletter overnight. You need to think it through—and plan out many of its attributes well in advance. If you like the idea of a newsletter and want to use it to network your business, here are ten questions to ask yourself:

1. What will be the purpose of the newsletter?
2. Who is the target audience?
3. Why would my target audience want to read it?
4. How will it benefit my audience?
5. What features will it contain?
6. Who will write the text?
7. Will I use a professional to design the layout?

8. How often will it go out?
9. How will it be distributed?
10. How will people sign up for it?

In order for a newsletter to be effective at networking your business, it should be of value to your audience. Why else would people spend their free time reading it? It should be informative and educational, like your presentation (see Week 34). It should motivate people to want to read it. It should make people talk about it and look forward to receiving it. You want people to use it productively—and that doesn't mean on the floor of a birdcage.

It's a mistake to turn out a newsletter that doesn't reflect well on your business. Whether printed on paper or contained in an e-mail, your newsletter needs to reflect your brand and image. Is it well written and easy to understand, or is it full of typos, jargon, and bad grammar? Is it well organized, attractively designed, and clearly printed, or is it a jumble of different type styles scattered on a photocopied sheet of construction paper? Is it produced with your audience in mind, or is the print too small for your mostly retired customers? If it's e-mailed, is it a downloadable, printable document that looks the same to everyone, or is its appearance subject to the mercy of different users' hardware and software whims?

> **Whether printed on paper or contained in an e-mail, your newsletter needs to reflect your brand and image.**

Unless you have a publishing or Web design expert on staff, you should seriously consider outsourcing the production of your newsletter to a professional—preferably someone in your network. Your newsletter is an extension of your business, a stand-in for you when you can't be everywhere. It's often the first thing a prospect sees of you. Would you show up in jeans and a T-shirt for a business meeting with a new client? You might, but you shouldn't expect to get the business.

Today, electronic newsletters are becoming more and more popular. How many have you signed up to receive? How many have you not signed up for but find yourself getting anyway? Determine how people will actually sign up to receive your newsletter. Equally important, how will they unsubscribe if necessary? Making it easy to unsubscribe helps keep your newsletter from being looked at as junk mail or spam.

Publishing a newsletter week after week or month after month is time-consuming and requires a strong commitment, but it can be a powerful networking and marketing tool. You want your audience to come to expect it—indeed, to look forward to receiving it—and that means you have to deliver it on time and with top-notch quality. An expert produces nothing short of the best.

Week 35 Action

Your task this week is to talk to someone who is producing a regular newsletter. Ask him or her the questions listed at the beginning of this chapter; his answers may give you valuable insight into the benefits, challenges, successes, and struggles of producing a newsletter. In the end, you need to determine whether the effort and cost of publishing a newsletter will produce an adequate return on your investment.

Write a Press Release

NEXT TO WORD OF MOUTH, publicity is the most cost-effective strategy you can use to market your business. It increases your credibility and helps you position yourself ahead of your competition—as long as it's positive publicity, of course.

First, it's important to understand the difference between advertising and publicity. The main objective of advertising is to gain new customers. You write the ad; you control the content, and often the placement, of your ad; you pay for it. Today's savvy readers know this. That's why people are skeptical of ads; they know you're selling to them.

By contrast, the main objective of publicity is to announce or inform. Publicity is usually free; in most cases, you don't have to pay to get your press release into the paper. You (or a professional writer) draft the press release, but someone at the paper edits it and turns it into an article before it's published, so you have no real control over what finally appears in print. Your ability to write a compelling, newsworthy press release helps to determine whether your announcement gets noticed and ultimately considered for publication. Most readers are less skeptical of articles; they assume that newspapers print only information that's newsworthy.

The main objective of publicity is to announce or inform.

We know from long experience working with business professionals that most people don't use all the press release opportunities available to them. Does that sound like you? If so, it's probably because (1) you're not sure if something is newsworthy, (2) you don't know how to write a press release, or (3) you don't have time to do it. Let's take a look at each of these issues and discuss how to deal with them.

How can you tell if something is newsworthy? First, you have to be very honest with yourself. Do you truly believe your community urgently needs this information about you or your business? Second, you have to put yourself in the reader's shoes. Would your next-door neighbor, the parents of your children's playmates, and/or the patients in your dentist's office be interested in reading this information? Why? Third, you have to put yourself in the editor's shoes. His interest is in satisfying his readers. He will publish your stuff only if it meets the "sniff test." If it smells like self-promotion or mindless fluff, your press release will be trash-canned in a nanosecond.

How many times has your business had something newsworthy to share with the community? How many times have you announced your accomplishments through the press? Press releases can be a great way to promote and network your business—when used responsibly and prudently. Is your company moving to a new location? Opening a second location? Introducing a new product? Celebrating an anniversary? Hiring more staff? Holding a grand-opening event? Sponsoring a charitable function? Celebrating significant growth? All of these examples are newsworthy. Your primary objective with a press release is to make an announcement. It is not to gain new customers—although if you gain a few, you won't complain—nor is it to crow about all the sales you made last week.

> **Your primary objective with a press release is to make an announcement. It is not to gain new customers—although if you gain a few, you won't complain.**

Perhaps you're not quite sure how to write a press release. Fear not. There are many online resources available to teach you how to structure, design, and format your press release. Here are twelve handy tips for writing great press releases (excerpted from www. press-release-writing.com):

1. Attract your reader with your title.
2. Provide an interesting angle.
3. Tell about your products or services in one or two clear sentences.
4. Use timely information, preferably related to current events or trends.
5. Deal only with the facts; avoid fluff.
6. Make it lively by using active verbs.
7. Limit adjectives, adverbs, and jargon.
8. Follow rules of grammar and style as you would for any piece of writing.
9. Don't write more than one page unless absolutely necessary.
10. Make every word count, and count every word.
11. Include ample contact information: name, address, phone, after-hours phone, fax, e-mail, Web site.

12. Make sure your release gets broad coverage with national and regional publications, radio and television stations, Internet publications, and all potential clients.

Once you've written a press release, how do you submit it, and to which publications? You'll find a handy resource at www.PRWeb. com, a member-supported, online press release distribution service, whose mission is to ensure that every organization, regardless of size, has access to the media. If you'd rather not utilize a membership service, use your network to connect locally with people who review press releases for your community's publications.

Finally, if you know your business can gain visibility and credibility with a press release, but you don't have the time or interest to write it yourself, hire a pro. A freelance professional writer can put together a compelling press release that will capture the attention of an editor, perhaps one with whom she's already developed a relationship, which increases your chances of getting it published. Professionals recommend that your business generate a press release once per quarter to remain visible in your industry and community.

> **Professionals recommend that your business generate a press release once per quarter to remain visible in your industry and community.**

Week 36 Action

Your task this week is threefold. First, brainstorm a topic for a press release. What's going on with your business that people need to know about? Second, search for press release templates and formats, and be sure to use the twelve tips listed above. If you're not comfortable writing your own press release, ask your network to refer you to a freelance professional writer. Third, schedule into your calendar a quarterly reminder to write the next press release. Networking your business is more than just going out and shaking hands; your business also needs to generate publicity—when it's deserved—to increase your visibility and credibility. And if you're serious about results, be sure to track the outcomes of your press releases.

☑ WEEK 37

Write Your Own Identity

RECENTLY, AN ASSOCIATE OF OURS who had read one of Ivan's books and attended some of his training sessions called Ivan and said, "I really love your material, but why don't you put more emphasis on your ideas about 'creating your identity as a brand' and how it affects your networking efforts? These ideas have made a huge impact on my business, but I don't hear you talking about it very often."

Ivan admitted this associate was right. He hasn't talked a lot about identity in his material, and he agrees that he should say more. Why hasn't he? You'll learn at the end of this week's strategy.

When Ivan started his first business decades ago, he had no idea how important it was to focus on branding his company and himself in the marketplace as a way of enhancing his networking efforts. He understood the concept from an advertising and marketing perspective, but with a small business he didn't have the advertising budget to mold himself or his company into any kind of brand—at least, that's what he thought at the time. So he ignored it. Big mistake, he realized later. It wasn't until the early '90s that he started to think about branding and how it would help in his networking efforts.

Networking is all about relationships. Relationships are about establishing credibility. Credibility takes time. What Ivan needed to do was expedite that process as much as possible while still creating genuine credibility in the marketplace at large. Not having much of a budget, he had to get creative about how he would make this happen.

Ivan saw that if he wanted to increase his visibility and enhance his credibility in the community, he needed to be viewed as the local expert. The way he decided to start creating that brand was to begin writing articles. Now, you may say, "What's so special about that idea? I've heard people suggest it before." Well, here's the bottom line: hearing it and doing it tend to be very different things.

You can derive the same identity-building, brand-boosting benefit from writing articles as Ivan did. It may surprise you, but editors and reporters need good story ideas and will use them wherever they can find them. Think about the things you know and understand best. What elements of that knowledge might be of interest to the general public, a specific industry, or some targeted demographic? Review the types of media outlets that write for your chosen audience. Consider newspapers, magazines, and industry journals, but also take a good look at online opportunities such as e-zines, online newsletters, and information sites (for example, www.Entrepreneur.com).

Editors and reporters need good story ideas and will use them wherever they can find them.

Either by phone or by letter, tell the editor why readers will be interested in the feature idea you have or why it is newsworthy. What are you doing in your business that strikes a chord in the community? What can you share that will educate the editor's readers? A word of caution, though: too many people who seek to be featured in newspapers or magazines send the equivalent of a company brochure. They fail to realize that editors and reporters need hooks, angles, ways to relate to a distracted, overworked, frenzied readership.

Guided by the Certified Networker training he took through the Referral Institute (www.referralinstitute.com), our associate chose a topic he knew about and worked with it for some time. He is in the travel industry, so he wrote a series of articles about travel and sent them to various outlets each month for several months. He received some responses—all "No, thank you"—until, finally, one local newspaper called him and said they'd like to use his piece in the next day's edition. After it came out, they contacted him again and asked if he'd like to do a monthly piece. Before long, another media outlet saw his work and asked him if he'd like to write for them.

Today he writes regular articles for several media outlets. More important, it has totally changed his business. Although most travel companies are going out of business due to vast changes in the industry, he is actually growing and thriving, because his articles have created an identity or brand for him and the company he owns. Moreover, he is still an active networker, and he notes that the articles he writes put him way above his competition by enhancing his credibility with the people he meets. He capitalizes on this regularly by bringing his recent articles to networking meetings.

This businessman's experience serves as a great example of what's possible for your own networking efforts. When you get some of your pieces published, promote them. They won't necessarily increase your sales overnight, but they will greatly enhance your credibility throughout the networking process, which absolutely increases your sales over time. Our friend also told us that he now includes links on his Web site to some of the online articles he produces as a way of enhancing his credibility with existing and potential clients.

So, if this is such a great idea, why hasn't Ivan said more about it? In his book *Masters of Success*, he talks about success being the "uncommon application of common knowledge."[1] If you ask a successful person the secret of his success, you will almost never hear a secret! Writing articles regularly and continually to increase your credibility and enhance your networking opportunities is not a secret. It's simply an idea that most people are just too lazy to implement.

> **If you ask a successful person the secret of his success, you will almost never hear a secret!**

The bottom line is, 98 percent of you won't actually do it. Or you'll do it for a little while and give up. The associate who encouraged Ivan to talk more about this strategy agreed, but he said, "Do it for the 2 percent of people like me who will apply the idea. It will make a difference for them, as it did for me."

Well, there you go. That's pretty good advice. So the question now is: Are you part of the 2 percent or the 98 percent? If you're part of the 2%, you're on your way to the 29%. If you're part of the 98%, you'll most likely stay in the 71%. Get it? It's your choice.

Week 37 Action

We encourage you to be in that 2 percent—if you believe you can stick with this strategy over time. Your task for this week is to sit down and jot down topics of four articles you could write that fit with your business and networking goals—and that you believe would serve the readers of a particular publication. Then, draft a letter addressed to the editor of that publication, and pitch your ideas. If he says yes, it's time to start writing! If the answer is no, consider following up with him to determine what kinds of articles would better fit his needs.

Here's a professional tip for ascertaining in advance what kinds of articles that publication might want: visit its Web site and check out the section devoted to prospective advertisers. Look for the publication's editorial calendar. It tells advertisers what themes will be covered each month or in each issue. Review that editorial calendar for topics that you could credibly write about.

If you are not an experienced writer, you may want to practice a bit before sending out your work. Make sure to have someone proofread at least your first few articles (the publications do have editors, but you will look more credible if you submit your articles free of major spelling and/or punctuation errors). You might also want to make sure your library includes such reference materials as a dictionary, a thesaurus, and at least one style manual (many publications use AP style).

SECTION SEVEN
CAPTURE YOUR SUCCESS STORIES

IN THIS SECTION we focus on four strategies that most people we know don't take full advantage of for their business: capturing success stories. This is understandable, for many of us are taught as children that we should be modest and self-effacing and that we should refrain from bragging about our successes. Such lessons are indeed wise for children. In fact, some adults we've seen have obviously forgotten those values. But there's a caveat to those rules that our parents usually didn't teach us: they apply to how we lead our individual, personal lives—not to our businesses.

Most of us dislike people who engage in a lot of puffed-up boasting, yet we are often quite intrigued by real-life business case studies or profiles that show how a company—even a one-person company—achieved success. Just imagine what would happen if such stories suddenly dried up. Business magazines and books would shrink to the size of pamphlets, and academic courses would meet from 10:00 to 10:05 a.m. No, success stories are far from taboo. They are vital for those of us dedicated to learning all we can learn in order to make our own enterprises as successful as possible.

Capturing your success stories involves being alert to how much your customers or clients have gained from using your products and services. Your success stories belong to you and are unique to your products and services. They are stories that come from your raving fans, people you would love to have riding through town like Paul Revere—not shouting a warning but singing your praises. Let's look at these four approaches to capturing your success stories.

Capturing your success stories involves being alert to how much your customers or clients have gained from using your products and services.

The Week 38 Strategy ("Ask for Written Testimonials") is about getting satisfied customers or colleagues to write letters on their own letterhead to spotlight their positive experience with you and your business. Such letters can be used in various ways to encourage other people to become your customers.

The Week 39 Strategy ("Write Down Two Success Stories") asks you to highlight your successes to help your network understand who best represents your preferred client. These stories should clearly emphasize what you do better than anyone else.

The Week 40 Strategy ("Write a Personal Introduction") shows you how to provide your network with material they can use when talking about you and your business with people who fit your preferred client profile. You don't want your sales force making stuff up about you, right? This simplifies their task—and ensures accuracy.

The Week 41 Strategy ("Toot Your Own Horn") encourages you to tell people about the good things your business does. This isn't about crowing over your amazing golf handicap or compli-menting your own fine taste in silk ties. It's about spotlighting your business's strengths, as well as its legitimate good works in the community.

Taking the time to implement each of these strategies could bring you opportunities to network your business far beyond the playing field of the typical networking arena.

☑ WEEK 38

Ask for Written Testimonials

WRITTEN TESTIMONIALS influence our actions and choices in myriad ways, sometimes without our even thinking about them. For example: You and a friend decide to catch a movie on Friday, but your tastes don't always coincide. So, you open the local paper and, together, check out the film reviews written by the paper's resident movie critic. You decide you want to go to dinner first, but there are so many restaurants in your area that you don't know which one to pick. So, you open up a local magazine that always features restaurant reviews, and you scan the recommendations of the magazine's food critic.

Even more powerful than these "professional" testimonials, however, are those that come from trusted personal contacts. If you have enough time, you might call or e-mail a couple of other friends to get their movie and restaurant suggestions. You're likely to follow their advice, too, because you know that they know your likes and dislikes pretty well.

So it is in business. Before people come to your firm for a particular product or service, they often want the comfort of knowing what others have said about you. Let's say you refinish hardwood floors. Many consumers, before they let you haul your refinishing equipment into their house, will ask you for either written testimonials or phone numbers of people who can attest to your work. You may even have experience with another form of testimonial: providing references when applying for a new job. Those references are expected to respond by written or spoken word about you and your work performance; quite frequently, a testimonial can clinch the job for you. That's a lot of weight riding on someone else's words!

Testimonials carry a level of credibility because they come from someone who has direct experience with your product or service. Consumers generally place more trust in a testimonial from another consumer than in a business's own marketing message. They believe that the average person is unbiased and has nothing to gain from providing a testimonial. The business stands to gain—or lose—everything, so its own words are seen as less trustworthy. Although most businesses are truthful with their customers, it's not hard facts but consumers' perceptions that drive their decisions.

Recognizing consumers' skepticism, some businesses make a practice of asking for customer testimonials. Ditto for businesses that serve other businesses. If anything, a business can be an even more demanding customer than an individual consumer, because it has its own reputation and ability to function at stake. Thus, a written testimonial on professional letterhead from one business to another is a powerful word in your favor, especially if the business represented on that letterhead is itself highly credible.

Have you ever asked a satisfied client for a written testimonial? We recommend making this standard practice for your business. Written testimonials can be used in many ways to enhance your credibility and set you above your competition—your business's Web site, for example. Some Web sites have them strategically sprinkled throughout so there's at least one testimonial on each page. Others have a dedicated page where a browser can view several testimonials at once. Both designs have their advantages.

Either way, scan each testimonial to keep it with its letterhead. This will enhance its credibility—and yours.

If your business attracts a lot of walk-in clients, it's helpful to display your written testimonials, each encased in a plastic sheet protector, in a three-ring binder labeled "What our customers say about us" or "Client Testimonials." Keep this binder on a table in your reception area, where your customers can browse through it while they're waiting for services. It's a good way to connect with your prospects and enhance your relationship with current clients.

Another way to stand out from the competition is to include testimonials with your business proposals. This strategy works best if you have a wide variety to choose from; you can include a selection of testimonials that are most relevant to a specific proposal.

Here are three keys to successfully using written testimonials:

1. Ask for testimonials at every opportunity.

2. Guide the content of your testimonials.

3. Update your testimonials.

Make it standard practice to ask clients (or other contacts) for testimonials. At what point in the sales cycle should you ask? This is a tricky question, but in general, ask for no testimonial before its time—which may be before, at, or after the completion of a sale or project, depending on your client, your product or service, and your own needs. Let's say that one month before finishing a project, you call your client to ask how things are going. The client tells you that she's very happy with the results and that her life or business has changed for the better because of your product or service. At this point, your testimonial detector should be pinging loudly. It's the right time to make your pitch: "That would be a great thing for other people to know about my company. Would you be willing to write me a testimonial on your company letterhead by the end of the week?"

If the answer is yes, the next step is to coach your client in writing a testimonial that fits your needs. Ask her to tell why she chose to work with you, how she benefited from your products or services, how you solved a problem for her, and what other people should know about your business. What things are most people concerned about when using a business like yours? Ask her to address those issues. Don't be afraid to offer suggestions; you'll make it easier for her to write an appropriate testimonial, and the result will be more valuable for you.

Finally, review your testimonial file or binder at least every two to three years to identify testimonials that are no longer valid or credible. Specifically, you may want to discard or refile a testimonial that

- is from a company that's no longer in business;
- is/was written by someone who has left that company;
- represents a product or service that you no longer offer;
- has begun to turn yellow with age; or
- needs to be updated with new statistics from the customer.

> **Review your testimonial file or binder at least every two to three years to identify testimonials that are no longer valid or credible.**

Week 38 Action

Your task this week is—you guessed it—to ask for three written testimonials on company letterhead. Make it easy for your advocates: specify what you would like their testimonials to cover, based on what you know of their satisfaction or successes from using your product or service. Ask for them to be typed on company letterhead, signed, and submitted by a certain date. One more thing:

Remember the law of reciprocity? It works here too. If you want to truly motivate someone to write you a testimonial, write one for her first.

☑ WEEK 39

Write Down Two Success Stories

BEFORE TELEVISION THERE WAS RADIO. Before radio there were books. And before books there were storytellers. The power of a well-told tale, passed down from generation to generation and recited from memory over a campfire, is the power that brought people together and formed the beginnings of cultures that have lasted even to the present day. No matter what the medium—stone tablets, movies, grocery store tabloids, the Internet—the story is central.

A good story stays with people and compels them to share it with others. It's as true today as it was two thousand years ago—and it's especially true of success stories. Everyone likes to hear them; everyone likes to have one. And doesn't this align nicely with word-of-mouth marketing, where referrals are based on thousands of individual success stories? Every time one networker passes a referral to another, she is telling a story about a need fulfilled successfully or a problem solved effectively.

A good story stays with people and compels them to share it with others.

You can empower your network with success stories about your business—as long as those success stories are truthful, substantive, and compelling. First, however, you need to write them down so they can be told to other people. The key is to capture a truly compelling story—one that practically begs to be shared, one that the people in your network would actually have trouble keeping to themselves.

The best story is one that profiles your preferred client (from Week 3's Strategy), so that more people like him will find their way to you. How do you do this? Close your eyes; imagine the perfect customer for your business. What makes him a perfect customer? What are his needs? How did you help him? Why did he choose you over your competitor? Now imagine that you are a profiler for the FBI (see Week 31 Strategy: Become a Profiler for Your Business). Your job is to profile this perfect customer in story format so that other people can go out and find more just like him. That's exactly why this strategy is so important for networking your business.

The anatomy of a successful word-of-mouth story about your business is quite simple. It has a captivating beginning, an action-packed middle, and a happy ending. If you're expecting other people to act on your story or to share it, it must be a compelling story—and by all means must have a positive outcome. So let's plop a good story down on the dissecting table and take it apart; this will show you what you need in order to put together your own story.

A Captivating Beginning: Who. We began this strategy by asking you several questions about your perfect customer. In the beginning of a success story, your goal is to set the stage so that the listener will want to hear more. Your purpose is to lure him in for the juicy middle that lies ahead. It is at this part of the story that you profile your perfect customer and connect with the listener. Use demographics to further define your perfect customer. Business-to-business demographics might include size of company, location, number of employees, type of structure, industry, and other factors. Business-to-consumer demographics might include age, gender, education, location, income, and more.

The Action-Packed Middle: What and Why. In the middle of your story, your goal is to define what problem the customer was having that brought her to you. What bind was she experiencing? What was not going well for her? Why did she choose you over your competitors? What were her needs? By capturing this part of your story, you trigger the listener to think of other people he knows who might be suffering from the same problem.

The Happy Ending: How and When. The ending is like the stuff in the middle of an Oreo cookie: it's the best part! The happy ending will tell your listener how you solved the customer's problem. How did you help her? How is she better off now after working with you? When did you solve her problem? How long did it take? This part of the story, the results, will typically get repeated the most. People want to know the results, the bottom line. They want to hear the facts and figures.

Why should you write these stories down? If your memory is anything like ours, do it so you won't forget them. But by writing them down (and encouraging your networking partners to do so as well), you can also swap them with your referral partners. This helps you learn to identify each other's preferred clients, and it provides stories with positive results that you can tell others on your partner's behalf. Keeping these words and stories on file greatly helps you find and refer great business opportunities to each other. You can also embed your own stories into a personal introduction that you might write for yourself (see Week 40 Strategy), and if you're creative, you can include them in a presentation about your business to a new prospect. Best of all: top off your success story with a written testimonial by the perfect customer!

Top off your success story with a written testimonial by the perfect customer!

Week 39 Action

Your task for this week is not only to write two success stories using the basic anatomy of a story as your guide, but also to share these stories with someone on your word-of-mouth marketing team. In a true giver's sense, ask your referral partner to share one of her stories with you as well. It will help you better understand what the ideal client looks like for her. Be sure to focus your story on your perfect customer. The more stories you share with other people, the more of these high-quality referrals you will get as you continue to network your business.

☑ WEEK 40

Write a Personal Introduction

MOST PEOPLE KNOW the importance of making a good first impression (see Week 24 Strategy: Make First Impressions Count), but surprisingly few would-be networkers give much thought to the role of a personal introduction in forming that first impression. When you're getting ready to make a presentation and someone is introducing you, you've got a captive audience—even before you begin speaking. It's a perfect opportunity, often wasted, to network your business.

> **When you're getting ready to make a presentation and someone is introducing you, you've got a captive audience—even before you begin speaking.**

You can't afford to let this opportunity slip by—whether you're being introduced to a networking group or a general audience—without using it to help get your marketing message across. Allowing someone who is unprepared to speak for you, no matter how good his intentions, is to risk misinforming or confusing your audience right from the start. Your personal introduction is something you can—and should—control.

A first impression based on a poor introduction is hard to overcome: "Aren't you the guy who sells fire insurance?"

"No, I used to sell insurance, but now I'm a hazard consultant. I help businesses guard against accidental fires in the workplace."

"Oh, that's too bad. I met someone not long after your talk who could have used your services, but I must have misunderstood what it was that you did."

When people are not clear on who you are when you are introduced, they filter what you say through their own misconceptions and end up missing your message.

Referral groups often invite professionals to make short presentations about their industry—a situation that's tailor-made for networking your business. That networking starts with your introduction. Before you arrive, prepare some information about yourself that is specifically tailored for your audience and for the person who's going to introduce you.

A typical personal introduction lasts a minute or two (unless your résumé is four pages long and you've won the Nobel Peace Prize). It should tell the audience who you are, what your business is, and how you help people. You can liven it up and pique the audience's interest by including a brief success story or anecdote. Here's how coauthor Michelle Donovan might ask to be introduced:

> Please allow me to introduce Michelle Donovan, the Referability Expert. Michelle is the founder of Pinnacle Training Services and owner of the Referral Institute of Western Pennsylvania, located north of Pittsburgh. She is a certified instructor for the Referral Institute's Certified Networker program. In addition, she provides training and coaching for adult educators and personal coaching on referral marketing. She is an adjunct professor at

Penn State and a guest faculty member of the University of Pittsburgh's Katz Center for Executive Education. Her mission is to offer referral training and coaching to business professionals to enhance their referability for ultimate profitability. Recently, she helped a career coach double his weekly client base in two months through referral marketing. Please welcome Michelle Donovan.

This personal introduction gives the audience an overview of Michelle's business. It highlights her involvement with specific universities, which adds credibility. It includes a short summary of one of her success stories. That's a lot of information in one or two minutes! Even better, Michelle controlled her introduction's verbiage and ultimately its potential outcome: referrals.

Week 40 Action

Your task this week is to write a personal introduction for yourself. The following framework will help you structure your introduction.

PERSONAL INTRODUCTION FRAMEWORK

Name and business _____

What do you offer? _____

What are your credentials or major accomplishments? _____
_____

What is your mission statement or statement of purpose? _____
_____

Recently he/she helped _____
_____ to _____ , which re-
sulted in _____.

Keep in mind that a personal introduction is not a one-size-fits-all blurb. You must be prepared to modify your introduction to fit the audience. In addition, when you give a prepared introduction to someone to read on your behalf, it should be double-spaced, bulleted, and in type no smaller than 12 points. This will greatly help the reader's confidence and ensure that your introduction is read smoothly and clearly. After all, you are allowing this person, who may or may not know you well, to network your business. Your responsibility is to make it count and control what elements you can.

A personal introduction is not a one-size-fits-all blurb. You must modify your introduction to fit the audience.

Unfortunately, many people are hesitant to write their own introductions. Why is that, you may ask? After all, when you write your own introduction, you can make sure it is accurate and that none of your accomplishments are left out. The key word here is "accomplishments" . . . the reason for the hesitation is because many people have trouble writing wonderful things about themselves! If you are one who has trouble "tooting your own horn," you'll definitely want to pay special attention to the next strategy in the book!

☑ WEEK 41

Toot Your Own Horn

"HEY, THERE, HOW'S IT GOING? What's new? How's business?" How many times in a week does someone ask you a similar question? If you're like most people, it happens a lot.

Now take a minute to think of your typical response. Again, if you're like most people, you probably answer back, "Fine." Or, "Things are going great; I'm swamped!" Or, "Business couldn't be better!" This usually means one of two things: either (1) things really are great, or (2) things are lousy but you want people to believe things are great.

When you respond this way, what does the person who asked the question walk away thinking? Boy, Jerry sure must have a full plate. He sounds too busy to help Sue, so I think I'll refer her to someone else.

If only you could have read your friend's mind! You'd be running after him yelling, "Wait! I really do want Sue's business!"

A financial advisor we know learned this the hard way when one of her favorite clients said to her, "I could have sent you several new clients, but you gave me the impression that business was great and that you really didn't have time for more clients." Suddenly she understood that every time she gave a falsely upbeat response, she was shooting herself in the foot.

As aspiring master networkers, do we really want to let anyone leave our presence thinking we don't need new business? Obviously, the answer is a resounding "No!" Then why do we consistently respond to such questions in a manner that seems to close the door to opportunity? What impact is it having on our business? As mentioned earlier in the book, you're leaving money on the table.

> **As aspiring master networkers, do we really want to let anyone leave our presence thinking we don't need new business?**

Here's an alternative to this mundane and counterproductive conversational habit. We call it "horn tooting." That's right, horn tooting. Now, don't confuse horn tooting with bragging. Bragging is being arrogantly or pompously boastful. Horn tooting is simply making positive, factual statements about your business in a way that highlights your successes while leaving the door open for new clients. Its purpose is to share positive information about your business with people who may be in a position to refer you or promote you to others.

> **Horn tooting is simply making positive, factual statements about your business in a way that highlights your successes while leaving the door open for new clients.**

Here are some horn-tooting responses you might consider using the next time someone asks one of these questions:

Q: "How's it going?"

A: "Life is good right now. I just landed one of my biggest clients ever."

A: "I'm about to enter my slow season, so I'm starting to look for new opportunities."

A: "I can't complain. I'm about to franchise my business."

Q: "What's new?"

A: "I'm really excited—I just hired a new salesperson."

A: "I was interviewed last week for the *Business Times*. It should be out in two weeks."

A: "I'm involved in a course right now that's teaching me how to shorten my sales cycle!"

Q: "How's business?"

A: "I've got eight new clients so far this year, but my goal is to get twenty."

A: "Sales are up 50 percent. I hope to hire someone new next month."

A: "Our third quarter was pretty good, but we're expecting to increase our client base even further in the fourth quarter."

These responses accomplish a few things for you and your business: (1) they inform the person of your accomplishments in a positive manner; (2) they provide information that can be repeated by someone on your behalf; and (3) they let people know how they can help you with your business. If you're in the habit of answering the "How's business?" question with a Pollyannaish comeback, try using something more in line with the above responses. As we said in the Week 32 Strategy ("Become a Motivational Speaker for Your Business"), it's all in the delivery.

Week 41 Action

Your task this week is to write two responses to each of the following questions and commit them to memory. The next time someone asks you a question of this sort, you'll be prepared to represent your business positively while inviting new opportunities. If you don't toot your own horn, who will?

Q: "How's it going?"

A:_____

A:_____

Q: "What's new?"

A:_____

A:_____

Q: "How's business?"

A:_____

A:_____

Throughout Section Seven, we have offered several suggestions for capturing—and using—your success stories. Once you are comfortable with this, you are already a big step "ahead of the crowd" . . . and well on your way to being ready to tackle the next section!

SECTION EIGHT
DO WHAT OTHERS DON'T

TO MOST BUSINESSPEOPLE, networking is something you try when you're hurting for business. We prefer to think of networking as a primary strategy for generating business relationships that lead to more referrals. When done correctly, networking is a proactive strategy for business growth, not a reaction to slow business.

This book is all about being different when it comes to networking your business. Note that this final section, "Do What Others Don't," is the largest section in the book. That's because it's the single most important idea: Doing what others don't gives you an edge. It can position you head and shoulders above your competition. It helps you stand out in a positive way, and when you do, people are attracted to you and your business, and your success grows stronger, deeper, and more durable.

Doing what others don't gives you an edge.

This section focuses on eleven specific strategies designed to give you the edge (Weekly Strategies 42–52). Most people don't do these things, and if they do any of them at all, they don't do them very well.

In the Week 42 Strategy ("Ask for Feedback"), we discuss how to gather information for improving your business. Getting straightforward feedback from people is the quickest way to identify your business's strengths and weaknesses so that you can take corrective action.

The Week 43 Strategy ("Adopt a Host Mentality") looks at how to stand out at a networking mixer in a positive way, by adopting the attitude of a host.

The Week 44 Strategy ("Follow the Money Trail") shows you how to capitalize on the support you give to other businesses.

The Week 45 Strategy ("Write a Letter of Support") explains how you can use your influence and professional status to help a member of your network solve a problem.

The Week 46 Strategy ("Ask for Referrals") teaches you how to ask for referrals (there truly is a better way).

The strategies in the middle of Section Eight take you outside the box. These include the Week 47 Strategy ("Read the Paper, with Referral Intent"), the Week 48 Strategy ("Conquer Your Fear of Public Speaking"), the Week 49 Strategy ("Become the Hub Firm of a Power Team"), and the Week 50 Strategy ("Become a Networking Mentor"). These strategies take ordinary activities and transform them into extraordinary ways to enhance your networking.

Finally, this section closes with two strategies that could strongly enhance the direction, growth, and development of your business. The Week 51 Strategy ("Recruit an Advisory Board for Your Business") focuses on the benefits of getting another perspective on your business from a team of volunteer advisors. The Week 52 Strategy ("Commit to Lifelong Learning") shares some information on where and how business owners can continue to learn the art and science of networking and referral marketing.

So, if you're ready, let's start looking at ways to position yourself as the top competitor—the one who does what the others don't do.

☑ WEEK 42

Ask for Feedback

IN YOUR BUSINESS OPERATIONS, do you ask for feedback from clients or customers? What system do you use? How often do you ask? Whom do you ask? When do you ask? How do you ask?

Asking for feedback is a simple way to gather information for improving our businesses, but many of us never take the time to ask. Some of us get so wrapped up in the day-to-day running of the business that we fail to pause and ask people, "How are we doing?" Others are simply intimidated by the process—and afraid of what they'll hear.

There are five main reasons why we don't ask for feedback: (1) we're afraid the response will be negative; (2) we don't know who to ask; (3) we don't know when to ask; (4) we don't know how to ask; and (5) we don't want to take up other people's time. With all these objections, the thought of asking for feedback can give us heartburn, but it's worth the pain; the potential for growth can be tremendous. Whether positive or negative, feedback should be considered constructive, because it helps our business develop new products, improve existing services, and sometimes adopt a whole new approach. This strategy is designed to help you integrate feed-back opportunities into the way you do business.

> **Whether positive or negative, feedback should be considered constructive, because it helps our business develop new products, improve existing services, and sometimes adopt a whole new approach.**

Fear of a negative response may be what stops most of us from embracing feedback. Nobody is eager to be criticized, especially self-driven, competitive businesspeople. Asking for feedback makes us feel vulnerable, and feeling vulnerable scares us. It's our built-in fear of rejection that makes us respond defensively: "Why didn't they like me? What's wrong with my products and services? What do they know, anyway?" This is the reaction of someone who is not ready to accept feedback.

> **As difficult as it can be to receive, negative feedback is actually a gift.**

As difficult as it can be to receive, negative feedback is actually a gift. It's a reality check; it reminds us that no matter how good we are, we can always improve. It's also a reminder that we can never truly make every person happy. Being willing to ask for feedback will indeed invite negative feedback on occasion. It's your attitude toward how you receive it that will turn negative feedback into a positive opportunity. You shouldn't ask for feedback unless you're ready to hear it—and respond to it constructively.

**You shouldn't ask for feedback unless you're ready
to hear it—and respond to it constructively.**

Whom should you ask for feedback? One answer is "every-body," exemplified by the 360-degree evaluation, a method commonly used in human resource management to gather feedback on an employee's performance. This evaluation broadens your perspective on work performance, because it involves a sampling from every type of person you come into contact with during your daily tasks—feedback from supervisors, coworkers, subordinates, partners, and customers, among others. Think of how this would apply to gathering feedback on the performance of your business. Whom might you include in a 360-degree evaluation? Perhaps you would consider external customers, internal customers (your staff), business advisors, and vendors. Gaining multiple perspectives on your business will ultimately give you a competitive advantage. In essence, having 360-degree vision will let you see things coming from all angles; without it, you may not see what's about to pounce on your business from behind! But you have to be ready to accept and apply the feedback.

When is the best time to ask for feedback? That depends on where you are in the process and what kind of feedback you're looking for. A professional development trainer, for example, will often ask for feedback in the middle of a session, at the end of a session, and three to four months after a session. He will ask different questions at different times—and the responses will differ. Based on the information he gets in the middle of the session, the trainer can adjust the material or delivery for that class. The feedback he receives at the end of the session may prompt him to modify the course for a future class. And input he receives several months after the class may give him information he can use in testimonials or to further improve the course.

What if you don't know how to ask for feedback? The easiest and most logical way is to make it part of your sales process. First, consider when you would like to ask for feedback. Like the trainer, would you want a multistage feedback system, or just a simple, one-time shot? Many companies use a questionnaire; some hand it out upon completion of the assignment, some e-mail it afterward, and some mail it as a follow-up in a few weeks. How you choose to deliver it depends on your product and customer base. Would your customers be more likely to return an e-mail than to snail-mail your questionnaire back to you? Knowing your customers helps you choose how to deliver your feedback opportunity; knowing your product helps you choose when. Regardless, it's time to give serious consideration to this strategy and how it could impact your business's growth.

The last reservation is that a lot of us are reluctant to take up someone else's time by asking for feedback. Quite frankly, this is a cop-out. Adults have the option of saying no—but it's still your responsibility to make the request. To increase the likelihood that you will get useful feedback, make the request simple and timely. If it's too complicated, or if you set a hurry-up deadline, your questionnaire will probably end up in the circular file. But don't set the deadline too far off, or people will lay it aside and forget it.

Our recommendation: begin integrating a feedback process into your sales system and into either your year-end evaluation or next year's planning session. Making it an integral part of your systems will help eliminate your fear that your request will be perceived as an imposition. Ultimately, your business will benefit from the value produced by feedback.

Begin integrating a feedback process into your sales system.

Week 42 Action

Your task this week is threefold: (1) review your sales system to determine when you can ask your clients for feedback; (2) create a simple tool (e.g., survey or e-mail questionnaire) to capture that feedback; and (3) search the Internet for samples of 360-degree evaluation tools to consider for the future. Remember the value of perspective locked inside a 360-degree feedback tool, and also remember the commitment needed to implement it successfully.

☑ WEEK 43

Adopt a Host Mentality

AT A TYPICAL NETWORKING EVENT, most people look and sound the same. Everyone seems to be there for one reason: to get business. Even so, you're not likely to make a deal at a networking function.

Why? Because most of the people there don't know you, or at least not well enough to conduct business with you. They certainly have no reason to trust you. They might not even like you—especially if you're cramming their pockets full of business cards. So, unless they're desperate and have been looking for someone like you for a long time, why would they refer anyone to you?

People need to know you, like you, and trust you before they'll refer you—and that includes referring their own business to you. But until you do something that sets you apart, you're just another desperate networker, hungry to make a sale—or maybe you're there for the grilled shrimp.

Wouldn't it be great to stand out positively at a networking function? To be the kind of person toward whom people gravitate at any gathering? The one everybody finds fascinating and wants to be introduced to? Well, there's a way you can achieve this, and it doesn't require surgery or the keys to a Lamborghini. It's simply this: behave like a host. Easy, but effective. If you adopt a host mind-set, people will naturally seek you out.

If you adopt a host mind-set, people will naturally seek you out.

Think about the last time you hosted a party. Were you a good host? If you were, you welcomed people at the door, introduced folks to one another, told them the plan for the evening, and went out of your way to see to their comfort. Your purpose was to help everyone else at the party have a good time.

It works the same in a networking environment. Most people you see at a networking event are playing the role of the guest. They are passive, waiting for something to happen. They're not sure who will be there. They're not sure what's on the agenda. They are curious to see who does what—and perhaps nervous about meeting new people.

You, on the other hand, can choose to do what other people don't do. You can shift your mind-set and approach a networking event as a host. If you do this, your actions change right from the start. You arrive early, so that you can learn the schedule for the event. You scan the list of attendees to find out who you can expect to see. You study the layout of the room so you can direct people to the coat closet, bathrooms, and food. You introduce people to each other and help them feel at ease. In other words, you take the initiative.

When you act this way, people are drawn to you. You seem to know everything about the event. You hear other guests say, "Go ask her." Your intentions change; your focus shifts from yourself to others. You demonstrate one of the most important traits of a master networker: helpfulness. You enjoy helping others (see Week 7 Strategy). You don't expect to get business from the event. Instead, you expect to meet people with whom you'll want to develop a deeper business relationship down the road. In doing so, you'll help others as well. When you implement this strategy, people will not only remember you, they'll like you because of your willingness to help them. This is the true meaning of networking. This is where it begins.

> **Change your mind-set and adopt a host mentality at the next networking event you attend. Arrive early to meet the people in charge. Learn the layout and flow of the event. Find out who is expected to attend. Make it your purpose to give of yourself and to help others.**

Week 43 Action

Your task this week is to change your mind-set and adopt a host mentality at the next networking event you attend. Arrive early to meet the people in charge. Learn the layout and flow of the event. Find out who is expected to attend. Make it your purpose to give of yourself and to help others. Set a goal to introduce three people to someone they don't know. The law of reciprocity will kick in, and in the long run you will reap the benefits.

Follow the Money Trail

HOW MANY BUSINESSES would you say you've supported over the years by being a loyal customer? Why, you may have been solely responsible for the new wing your veterinarian added to her office last year, just from all the money you've invested in your pet's care over the last ten years. For some businesses, not only may you have been a customer—you may also have recommended them to other people. When was the last time those businesses returned the favor and helped your business succeed? This strategy—following the money trail—shows you how to leverage the law of reciprocity with the businesses you have financially supported.

Before you get deep into this strategy, go find your checkbooks—both personal and business. We'll wait . . . There, now that you have your checkbook(s) in front of you, it's time to follow the money trail. Scan your checkbooks for local businesses that you have paid. You may notice regular expenditures, such as your hairstylist, veterinarian, physician, lawn care service, housecleaning service, dry cleaners, day care, pet resort, or grocery store.

First, let's put this money trail into perspective. Start by analyzing just how much you have invested in these businesses. The following table will help you.

FOLLOW THE MONEY TRAIL

Instructions: List every business where you've regularly spent money over the last year. In the next column, list how frequently you made an investment. In the last three columns, list the amounts you invested in one month, one year, and five years.

Business Name	Frequency of Investment	Total Invested for 1 Month	1 Year	5 Years
Example: Salon Supreme	Once a month	$40	$480	$2400

Reviewing these figures will help you realize just how much you've invested toward the success of some of your favorite businesses. Staggering, isn't it? Now, what can you do with this information?

The law of reciprocity states that if I help you, you will, in time, help me in return. We would venture to guess that most of these establishments have never been approached by their customers with a request of reciprocity. What would you say to them? How would they react? Why bother? You might wonder: What could a hairstylist do for me—or for a financial planner—other than style hair? Or, what could a veterinarian do for a carpet cleaner?

Seeking reciprocity begins with your willingness to ask the question. Your request needs to be specific and needs to be supported by how much you have invested in their business over the last year or so. Are you willing to approach your favorite businesses and ask them to support your business in some way? If yes, let's start with these two examples and then consider what you could do for your own business.

What could a hairstylist do for a financial planner? Stylists have patrons, who mostly sit in the waiting area or in styling chairs, with not much to do but read. Wouldn't it be nice if your newsletter was there to help them pass the time? Wouldn't it be lovely to have ads in the salon's own quarterly newsletter?

First, the financial planner needs to take the hairstylist—let's call her Joan—to lunch or coffee and engage her in conversation:

> Financial planner: Thank you for joining me for lunch. I wanted to get some time with you away from the salon so I could talk with you about your business—and to ask for some help with my own business. I've enjoyed being your client for the last five years, and I'm glad I was able to refer four other people to your salon who have become clients. I wanted to ask if you might be willing to help support my business as well.
>
> Joan: I have very much enjoyed you as a client, and I do appreciate your referrals. What did you have in mind?
>
> Financial planner: As a client, I receive your quarterly newsletter. I see that you often have advertisements from community businesses. Would you give me space in your newsletter for an ad for one year?
>
> Joan: Sure, but that would cost about $500 for the year.

Financial planner: I was hoping that you would give me the space for no charge in return for my past referrals and for being such a loyal customer, even after moving twenty miles away.

Joan: I see your point. No one has ever asked me to do anything like this before. But it makes sense to me, since you are actively supporting my business. The least I could do is give you ad space. Sure. I'd be happy to help you. Is there anything else you'd like me to do?

Financial planner: As a matter of fact, there is. Could I leave one of my newsletters in your waiting area for your patrons to read while they wait?

Joan: That would be no problem.

In this example, Joan was willing and able to help the financial planner expand her visibility. Most people, once it is pointed out to them, understand that the law of reciprocity goes both ways. If they seem reluctant to help you, it's time to reconsider your loyalty. Should you continue to support someone else's business when he or she flatly refuses to help your business in return?

Most people, once it is pointed out to them, understand that the law of reciprocity goes both ways.

Here's another example: What could a veterinarian do for a carpet cleaner? The carpet cleaner looks for clients who have pets, because pets sometimes have accidents on carpets. Wouldn't it be great if every person who visited the vet's office could read or take home a pamphlet from the carpet cleaner? Or read an article about new puppies and carpet care in the vet's monthly client newsletter? The vet would actually be providing value to his clients by sharing information on the carpet cleaner's business. Here's how you might handle this conversation:

> Carpet cleaner: I want to thank you for taking a few minutes to meet with me. I've been your client now for about three years and have been impressed with the care you give my pets. I even sent three of my family members to you last year. Would you be willing to support my business in return?

> Veterinarian: Well, that depends on what you have in mind. What do you do?

> Carpet cleaner: My business is cleaning carpets, and I'm looking for home owners in this area with several pets. Would you let me write an article for your next newsletter on how people can protect their carpets after they get a new puppy? It would give me great visibility and probably save you some time.

> Veterinarian: Actually, that's not a bad idea. It's perfect timing, since a lot of people get new puppies in the spring. And, to tell you the truth, I would love for someone else to write an article or two instead of having to do them all myself. I'm getting very busy, and the newsletter takes up a lot of my time. Can you have something to me by the end of the month?

Should you continue to support someone else's business when he or she flatly refuses to help your business in return?

In both of these situations, the person being asked probably never had a customer make a request like this before. If a loyal customer and a cold caller approached them with the same request, who do you think would get the nod? As a client, you're giving a lot to someone else's business. It's not unreasonable to ask for something that supports your business in return.

As a client, you're giving a lot to someone else's business. It's not unreasonable to ask for something that supports your business in return.

Now think about your business, and about the businesses you support. What can you ask of them? Can you contribute to their newsletter? Will they display your pamphlet? Will they post your business announcements? Can you leave a stack of business cards on their coffee table? Will they pass out your business's coupons to their customers at the register? Will they sponsor your next event?

Week 44 Action

Your task this week is, first, to complete the worksheet we provided earlier in this strategy. Next, approach one establishment for help with promoting your business, following the suggestions in these examples. After all, when you follow the money you've spent at other people's establishments, isn't it about time some of it came back around to you?

When you follow the money you've spent at other people's establishments, isn't it about time some of it came back around to you?

☑ WEEK 45

Write a Letter of Support

WE HAVE MENTIONED THROUGHOUT THIS BOOK that word-of-mouth marketing depends on quality relationships to succeed. People will not refer you if they don't know you, like you, and trust you. The trust factor is built on integrity and authenticity. People recognize when they are being sold to and when someone's intentions are not genuine. (Remember that sincerity and trustworthiness are two of the top ten traits of a master networker, as we discussed in the Week 7 Strategy.)

One of the strategies you can use to further develop a relationship is to write a letter of support that will help someone on your word-of-mouth marketing team in some way. Take note that this is not a testimonial letter, but a letter that provides influence and support on someone's behalf. For example, if you use your influence and professional status to help a team member solve a problem, gain political advantage on an industry issue, or support a cause that could dramatically affect his business success, your efforts won't go unnoticed. Your relationship with this person will grow stronger simply because of your professional support. The caveat: As always, your intention to help this individual must have integrity and authenticity.

Let's look at a couple of examples of how you might apply this strategy.

Imagine that you are a CPA, and many of your clients are small business owners in your county. You see an article in the paper about a bridge reconstruction project scheduled to begin in November and last through January—a bridge used by many of your clients' customers. As a CPA, you know that these clients rely heavily on their November and December business, and that closing the bridge will seriously diminish their annual revenue. You write a letter to the editor warning of the economic impact and asking the city government to postpone the project until spring. Several of your clients see the letter and call to thank you. If you're smart, here's what you say: "I felt it was the right thing to do. I'm sure your financial advisor would do the same." This could lead to a discussion of financial advisors and where to find them, giving you an opening to refer your colleague—the financial advisor. Beyond that, other business owners in the area who are not now your clients might decide to put you in their Rolodex. You've done a good deed, and gratitude can be expressed in many ways.

Now imagine that you're a mortgage broker who has strong relationships with several real estate agents. You read in a real estate journal that two months from now state regulators will hold public hearings on a proposal to require agents to pay for home staging services. If enacted, this regulation would slash agents' profits and make it harder to buy a home. You write a letter to the journal, expressing your concern and urging realtors to show up and testify against the rule. You mail copies of the letter to the real estate agents who give you business and to the other agencies in the area. You receive calls from many agents you know and others you don't know—all thanking you for your support. You have just added value to your current relationships and enhanced your reputation in the region as a mortgage broker who has his thumb on the pulse of the industry and cares about real estate agents.

There are some lessons to be learned here. The first is that most people read only the journals of their own industry. It's great to be up-to-date and informed in your industry; your clients would expect as much from a professional. But imagine your client's response when she sees that you are also well informed about what's going on in her industry. This positions you as an expert in your target market.

The second lesson is to react quickly and take the initiative. This is the perfect opportunity to practice being a catalyst (Week 16 Strategy). When you hear about an issue that affects your clients, show your support by getting involved on their side. Make sure others in the industry know it too—especially those you would like to have on your networking team or roster of clients.

When you hear about an issue that affects your clients, show your support by getting involved on their side. Make sure others in the industry know it too.

Week 45 Action

Your first task this week is to determine what your clients and prospects are reading and subscribe to one of those journals. How do you find out? It's easy: ask them. The next time you're in a client's office, look around. Ask for an old edition of the journal; tell him you'd like to be more informed about his industry.

Your second task is to ask your best clients what trends or issues they're facing now or expect to face in the near future. Offer them your support. Ask if it would be helpful for you to write a letter on their behalf to support their industry. Then do it.

☑ WEEK 46

Ask for Referrals

WHEN COUNSELING BUSINESS PROFESSIONALS, we're always amazed at how many have never asked their friends, associates, networking partners, customers, or clients for a referral. Most will say up front that, yes, they've asked for referrals, but when we've probed, we've found that they asked only a small percentage of their contacts and, getting no favorable responses, stopped trying.

Why do they get discouraged? In many cases, it's because they're asking in terms that are too general. Rather than describing their preferred client (see Week 31 Strategy: Become a Profiler for Your Business), they're making their request so unspecific that it doesn't connect with anybody in their contact's mind. The more specific you are in your request for a referral, the more likely it is that a specific person will come to mind.

Other networking experts have recognized the power of asking for particular kinds of referrals. Mark Sheer outlines a very effective approach in his book *Referrals*. He has found that the way you phrase the question is a key factor. He recommends something very close to this: "I'm expanding my business and I need your help. Who do you know who . . . ?"[1]

Mark goes on to say, "You must not alter this phrase. It has been tried and proven successful. Other phrases have been tried and have not produced the desired results—so don't waste your time using them. Once you become comfortable with this new phrase, it is very easy to ask your contact for a referral by simply saying, 'Who do you know who . . . ?'"[2]

This format allows people to think about specific ways they may be able to refer to you. Most people who do not get a positive response to their request fail because they have asked a very broad, closed-ended question, such as "Do you know anyone who needs my service?" That's too general. Your referral source can't possibly do a mental sort on everyone he knows and tell you who he thinks could use your services. Make it easier for him by narrowing it down.

Here's a great example of how this technique can be used. Ivan received a letter asking for referrals for an educational toy company. The letter gave some basic information about the company and then asked the following questions:

- Who do you know that is having a baby?
- Who do you know that is a new parent, grandparent, aunt, or uncle?
- Who do you know that needs developmental toys for their children?
- Who do you know that belongs to an organization that donates to children's groups?
- Who do you know that is a teacher?

By listing specific examples of your target market in this way, you help your referral prospect do a mental sort that is far easier than the general question "Do you know anyone who needs my service?" This seems to be counterintuitive to many businesspeople, like telling a boxer to lean into the punch: narrowing the field down doesn't sound like a good idea. But effective networkers have learned that the easier you make it for people to understand what you do, sort through their contacts, and think of a referral for you, the more referrals you will get.

> **The easier you make it for people to understand what you do, sort through their contacts, and think of a referral for you, the more referrals you will get.**

Week 46 Action

Your task this week is to write a letter or e-mail to your clients and send it out with three to five "who do you know who" questions that apply to your business. Furthermore, if you belong to a referral network, take this letter to the next meeting and use it as the basis of your presentation. Watch how being more specific with your requests generates more referrals.

Read the Paper, with Referral Intent

WHEN YOU FIRST GLANCE at the title of this strategy, you might say, "OK, how is reading the newspaper doing something that other people don't do? I know a lot of people who read the paper!" No doubt you do. Maybe you're one of them! The point is how you read the paper—and to what purpose.

Most folks read the newspaper to gain insight into local and world events and news—and that's all. We're suggesting that you read the paper differently—to look for opportunities for referrals.

A master networker within the 29% is, as we pointed out near the beginning of this book, a gatekeeper (Week 5 Strategy: Give to Others First). A gatekeeper is the person to whom others look when they have a problem to be solved or need information about something that affects them. By building relationships with the people in your network and being willing to help them grow their business by referring them, you position yourself as a gatekeeper— a solver of problems and a center of influence.

Pick up your local newspaper and scan the front page. Turn to the local section, then the business news, and then the lifestyle section. The paper is teeming with opportunities for you to act as a gatekeeper for the people in your network. Every page presents problems or significant issues of one kind or another. Remember how we said in the Week 7 Strategy that one of the top ten traits of a master networker is that he "works his network"? This means, among other things, that the master networker's eye is trained to see problems and opportunities where an ordinary reader might see only words.

The paper is teeming with opportunities for you to act as a gatekeeper for the people in your network.

Look again. What are people saying? Hear their voices. Who is talking about problems or changes in her company or industry? What is happening that could have a direct impact on you or someone in your network? Who is in need of the services of someone you know? Where are there networking opportunities for you and your marketing team?

The paper is a tremendous source of leads—information and resources that could be beneficial to you or to someone in your network. A lead should never be confused with a referral; however, with the right approach, a lead can be turned into a referral. Let's look at how this might happen.

A lead should never be confused with a referral; however, with the right approach, a lead can be turned into a referral.

One day, you're reading the paper and you see in a story that Bosworth, Bazooka & Blunderbuss Inc. has lost its lease in the Elysian Fields Industrial Park. Being the alert problem solver that you are, you hear yourself saying, "Wow, that's a huge endeavor.

I wonder who's going to handle that relocation." Instantly, you think, Linda! Linda is an expert project manager, who specializes in helping companies move. You think, I need to call Linda about this. (This is a lead for Linda, not a referral, because right now you don't know anyone at BBB Inc. to whom you could introduce Linda.) So you get on the phone and call Linda. You tell her about the story and simultaneously e-mail it to her from the paper's Web site. In the meantime, Linda, being an effective networker, begins to spread the word through her network to see if anyone can personally introduce her to someone high on Bosworth's org chart. In no time, Linda gets a hit on her request and quickly finds herself in front of the CEO—accompanied by one of the people in her network who happens to be the CEO's friend. (This is a referral.) Linda is hired for the job. Do you think Linda is grateful to you for keeping her in mind? Is she likely to do the same for you? Absolutely!

This opportunity for Linda came about because you were reading the paper with referral intent. The same thing can happen for you and your business. If you read something in the paper that sounds like a great business opportunity, remember: it's a lead, not yet a referral. Don't fall into the trap of cold-calling the company—you know how that's going to turn out (review Week 2 Strategy). Instead, start putting the word out to your network, the way Linda did. This strategy will increase the likelihood of finding someone in your network who can make the right introduction at the right time.

Week 47 Action

Your task this week is twofold: (1) read the paper, with referral intent for two people in your network, and find each of them an opportunity or a lead that they might capitalize on through their network; then (2) find your own business a lead or two on which you can capitalize, and begin to ask your network for help in making the connection for you.

☑ WEEK 48

Conquer Your Fear of Public Speaking

IN MANY SURVEYS OVER THE YEARS, people have ranked the fear of public speaking as worse than the fear of dying! Standing and talking to an audience can be frightening, especially if it's for more than a couple of minutes.

Unfortunately, no matter how hard you try to avoid it, networking your business is going to involve public speaking. You may find yourself giving a sixty-second elevator pitch at a networking meeting, a ten-minute presentation at a chamber function, or a forty-minute educational presentation to a prospect. As we mentioned in the Week 32 Strategy ("Become a Motivational Speaker for Your Business"), you've not only got to be comfortable with public speaking, but you also have to be motivational as well, because in word-of-mouth marketing, the message always begins with you. What most of us don't realize is that despite what our fears are telling us, the audience genuinely wants us to succeed.

No matter how hard you try to avoid it, networking your business is going to involve public speaking.

If you are truly paralyzed by the fear of speaking, we recommend that you seek professional assistance and guidance to help you manage your fear. For those of you who dread it but somehow find the strength to do it—despite the sweaty palms, racing heartbeat, and anxiety—we have a few tips from our experiences that might help reduce your stress.

1. Prepare, prepare, prepare! Don't wing it! Prepare an outline of what you want to say, and practice it. Use note cards, or type your remarks out on a piece of paper. (Print or type large. Make it ridiculously easy to read, so you don't lose your place in the paragraph.) Don't overprepare, though; this can just lead to more anxiety.

2. Be specific, and talk about the things you know best. At networking meetings, don't try to teach people everything you do in one short pitch. Think in terms of teaching the audience something of significance. Focus on just one or two areas of your business—the topics you feel you understand best. This will increase your comfort level and reduce stress.

3. Use handouts, visuals, or PowerPoint slides to support your presentation. If you're worried about stage fright, props such as books, slides, handouts, or gadgets will help you keep your mind on your topic, add a special element of interest to your presentation, and give the audience something to concentrate on besides you. PowerPoint can be a great tool, but it becomes a noticeable crutch if you fall into the trap of reading from the slides. PowerPoint should support your presentation, not be your presentation. Read a few of the many books and articles available on using PowerPoint.

4. Remember, you're the expert. It's true. In the eyes of the audience, you are the expert, and they want to hear what you have to say. They're eager to learn something from you. If you focus on what you know best, you will feel more confident and be more credible. Believe in yourself and in your message.

Remember, you're the expert.

5. Be creative. Find a way to communicate that makes you comfortable. Instead of talking to a group, engage them in conversation; or start with Q & A, and then answer at length. Don't be afraid to be different. Surprise your audience. Walk around the stage or up into the seats. People get tired of the same old approach and are invigorated by something unexpected. Have fun with your message; it will help you turn your nervous energy into positive energy. The audience will feel it and radiate it back to you, and before you know it, your anxiety is gone.

In BNI weekly meetings, members periodically get to deliver a ten-minute presentation about their business. One member, a CPA, asked if she absolutely had to do this. She was told it was expected of everyone; it helped the other members learn how to refer them effectively. At that point, she threatened to quit the organization. When asked why, she said that it took everything in her power just to stand and deliver a brief, sixty-second presentation. "If I have to speak for ten minutes, I'll simply have to quit. It's too stressful."

She was assured that no one would make her speak if she didn't want to. This seemed to alleviate her anxiety. The conversation continued, but the topic came up again, and the others tried to help her understand that she would be forfeiting the opportunity to educate members about what she did and the kind of referrals she needed. Yes, she said, but she couldn't handle the anxiety.

"Well then," someone asked, "how would you feel about coming up with ten true-or-false questions about tax law and small businesses? Could you just read the test questions and tell us the answers? That would help the other members."

She thought for a moment. "Yes, I could do that—as long as I don't have to give a speech." She was assured that no speech would be necessary.

On the day of her "non-speech," she started hesitantly. By the third question, however, she was becoming more and more animated. Before long she was digressing from her prepared questions and talking excitedly with her audience. She was professional, informative, and funny, and she was having a good time.

After fifteen minutes, the president gave her a nudge and asked her to wrap it up, because she was going over the allotted time. She was shocked. She had lost track of the time—because she had lost her fear. After all, she wasn't giving a speech!

This is what we mean when we suggest giving your presentation in a way that feels comfortable. Think creatively about what you know and how you like to communicate. You'll find that you don't have to pass up speaking opportunities that can strengthen your networking.

Take a look at some of the many books and tapes available on public speaking. *Masters of Networking* has an excellent contribution by Joe McBride. If you have this book, let's turn our hymnals to page 103 . . .

**Position yourself as the expert; enjoy the
satisfaction of educating other people.**

Week 48 Action

You can't get better at something if you never practice it! Your task this week is to go looking for opportunities to practice the above tips. If you're nervous, start small with your one-minute elevator pitch. Make it a point to fill the entire minute exactly. Work up to five- and ten-minute talks as you gain confidence. When you feel ready, look for an opportunity to make a lunchtime educational presentation. The program chairs of many associations and membership organizations are always on the lookout for speakers. Position yourself as the expert; enjoy the satisfaction of educating other people. When you remember to apply the tips in this strategy, we feel confident that it will alleviate much of your speaking anxiety. One final thought: It's good to be a little nervous. Just convert that into positive energy, and you'll have the audience in the palm of your hand.

☑ WEEK 49

Become the Hub Firm of a Power Team

THE WORLD'S BEST-KNOWN MARKETING SECRET defines a hub firm as "the key business in a constellation of independent businesses tethered to one another to make the most effective use of the organizational strengths of each."[1] To capture the image of a hub firm, imagine the spokes of a wheel, with one business positioned in the center—the hub—surrounded by other businesses with which it has very strong collaborative relationships. These businesses are your power team. Each collaborative relationship around the wheel has taken considerable time to develop. In a hub firm scenario, the business in the center of the wheel is the organizer of the inter-related parties or power team. The hub firm sets the wheel into motion as needed, per project, to benefit the customer. The cooperative relationship between these businesses can provide the hub firm with a significant competitive advantage over its competition. This is the true essence of a strategic partnership.

To become a successful hub firm, you must base the selection of your power team on the quality of your relationship. You must have a high level of trust in and credibility with each business, since you will be calling on their services to help your clients. In some cases, these businesses may come right from your specific word-of-mouth marketing team. They must also be chosen based on their ability to meet the current specific needs of your client. Imagine how much value you begin to add to those relationships when you position yourself as a hub firm. Let's take a closer look at the composition of two different hub firms and the kinds of projects that set the wheel in motion.

Hub Firm #1

The hub firm owner, a financial advisor, has surrounded himself with three other business professionals: a CPA, a business attorney, and a business banker. Every so often, the financial advisor finds himself in front of a client who is trying to start a business. The financial advisor could deal with the client's issues—financial investments, 401(k) plans, etc.—then turn him out into the world to find his own CPA, attorney, and banker. Or the financial advisor could activate his hub firm and approach the client with a comprehensive analysis of his financial situation. This would involve the CPA, the banker, the attorney, and the financial advisor, all working together as a package deal to help the client. The financial advisor thus becomes not just a financial advisor but a wealth of resources for his client. This strategy not only sets him above his competition, but it also saves his client an enormous amount of time (and money), since he has all the resources he needs right at hand.

Hub Firm #2

To set herself apart from her competition, a real estate agent builds a constellation of complementary firms around her: a photographer, an interior designer, a carpet cleaner, and a landscape architect. Whenever the real estate agent gets a listing, she activates this power team. The carpet cleaner starts by cleaning all the carpets in the house. The interior designer stages the home and provides suggestions to make the interior appealing. The landscape architect enhances the curb appeal. Finally, the professional photographer takes high-quality photos of the interior and exterior for marketing purposes. The team ensures that the client's home is in top condition, inside and out, for potential buyers. The real estate agent provides all of this as a service to the client. She could have recommended these businesses separately to the home owner, but she chose instead to provide a unified package of services. Serving as a hub firm not only sets her far above her competition, but it also adds exceptional value to the client by saving him time and money.

Both of these examples demonstrate the advantages of positioning your business as a hub firm. The key is finding the right businesses to surround you. You need not activate all of the businesses in your team for each project; instead, bring in selected businesses based on what you, as the hub firm, identify as the needs of the client.

Week 49 Action

Your task this week is to design a power team with yourself as the hub firm. Identify projects or clients you might better serve using the power team strategy. Which businesses would you involve? Who do you know in those businesses? How well do you know them? If you know them well enough, talk with them about collaboration. By becoming a hub firm, you make yourself and your business the key link in a special network of other businesses. Over time, you'll find yourself getting more and better referrals as you strengthen your relationships.

☑ WEEK 50

Become a Networking Mentor

CAN YOU REMEMBER SOMEONE who selflessly shared his wealth of knowledge and experience with you to help you succeed? Mentors come to us disguised as parents, coaches, teachers, colleagues, supervisors, and friends. Mentors share with us what they've learned in order to help us avoid making the same mistakes they made. They support us through our struggles with guidance and constant nurturing. They celebrate our achievements as if they were their own. They are the very embodiment of the "Givers Gain" philosophy.

Mentors are invaluable resources for our business success. They guide us through growth, change, and crisis; they help us become who we truly are meant to become. Mentors are leaders, often leading by example. Leaders move us forward. Peter F. Drucker says, "Leadership is lifting a person's vision to higher sights, the raising of a person's performance to a higher standard, the building of a personality beyond its normal limitations."[1]

Take a moment and tap into the feelings you have for your mentors. If you're like us, you feel a deep sense of gratitude, respect, and admiration for them. If you could, you would no doubt place them on a pedestal—not to mention thank them for all their help. This relationship will stand the test of time and distance. If a mentor called you today and asked for a favor, you'd stop what you were doing and give her request your full attention. You would do almost anything for her, with the utmost attention to details of service and quality.

Imagine that you were someone's mentor—and that person had those same feelings toward you. Imagine the depth and intensity of that relationship. Imagine the loyalty. Imagine the sense of accomplishment you'd feel. Perhaps there is someone who already considers you a mentor. Perhaps you know someone you'd like to mentor—someone who reminds you of yourself when you were just getting started in business.

It's common knowledge that if you want to improve your skill, then you should teach someone else. Ivan learned this firsthand many years ago in martial arts. He discovered that by teaching other students some of the fundamentals, he improved his own martial arts skills. Later, this lesson was repeated in chess. Ivan was always a decent player at the game. However, it wasn't until he started coaching a school chess club that his game really started to improve. Teaching young people the rudiments of chess strategy made him focus on improving his own game. Sometimes mentoring and coaching others gets us to focus on the basics and apply them better ourselves. After fifty weeks of learning and applying the concepts outlined in this book, it is time for you to start helping others with these strategies. It's time to reach back to someone stuck in the 71% of the population who are disconnected and begin to connect them to your network. This behavior embodies the qualities of those in the 29% of the population who are intimately connected to the world. In addition, this will definitely improve your networking skills by acting as a refresher for what you've learned and getting you to refocus your efforts on areas you may have forgotten.

Week 50 Action

This week, your task is to assess your own potential for becoming an effective mentor. Before entering into a mentoring relationship, however, you should reflect on each of the qualities of a good mentor presented in this list, courtesy of the Web site www.sonic. net/~mfreeman/mentor/mentchar.htm.

Characteristics of a Good Mentor

- A Desire to Help

  Individuals who are interested in and willing to help others.

- Have Had Positive Experiences

  Individuals who have had positive formal or informal experiences with a mentor tend to be good mentors themselves.

- Good Reputation for Developing Others

  Experienced people who have a good reputation for helping others develop their skills.

- Time and Energy

  People who have the time and mental energy to devote to the relationship.

- Up-to-Date Knowledge

  Individuals who have maintained current, up-to-date technological knowledge and/or skills.

- Learning Attitude

  Individuals who are still willing and able to learn and who see the potential benefits of a mentoring relationship.

- Demonstrated Effective Managerial (Mentoring) Skills

  Individuals who have demonstrated effective coaching, counseling, facilitating, and networking skills.[2]

After determining your interest in and capacity for becoming a mentor, you might want to take a look at those in your various networking circles who might benefit from your help or area of expertise. There are also many volunteering opportunities at local high schools or community colleges, where there are many students who could benefit from having a mentoring relationship at this time in their lives.

Keep in mind, though, that many potential "mentees" may be shy about approaching you, assuming you are too busy with your business to help them. Make your availability known, and you may soon be involved in one of the most professionally and personally fulfilling relationships of your life.

☑ WEEK 51

Recruit an Advisory Board for Your Business

YOU MAY ALREADY HAVE DISCOVERED that it's next to impossible, on your own, to keep up with all the information you need for maintaining and growing your business. There's just too much of it, and your own inclinations, skills, and time limitations steer you toward pursuing only certain kinds of knowledge. You may be strong in marketing and business planning, for example, but weak in personnel and legal matters. Is there a way to ensure that you're not neglecting important areas of your business while you're scrambling to keep up in others?

As a business professional, you also need a constant supply of information to achieve success. You must stay aware of trends and issues and keep up with rapid economic and technological changes to be competitive in your industry. You may feel that you're working too much *in* your business and not enough *on* your business. Is there a way to maintain a balance between day-to-day operations and the big picture?

In both cases, the answer is yes—the advisory board. Many successful businesspeople recruit an advisory board to keep them up to speed on fixing problems and running the business smoothly, while staying abreast of what's happening in the larger world of commerce, economics, and technology. When you form and consult with an advisory board, you are truly exhibiting one of the key traits of a master networker: you are working your network (see Week 7 Strategy).

An advisory board is a group of people from outside your business who can provide you with the knowledge and expertise you need to run a successful operation. The knowledge you lack is always someone else's specialty, so it makes sense for you to turn to others for help. When you set up an advisory board, you are creating a web of contacts who know and understand what you must do to achieve success in your profession or business, and who have the experience to help you achieve your goals. Your advisory board becomes a powerful asset for your business, a resource that can take much of the burden of working in your business off your back so that you can focus on your business.

An advisory board is not necessarily a group that you have to recruit for yourself. One variety of advisory board is the mastermind group, which is a lot like a business networking group, except that instead of networking for referrals, businesspeople from many different professions and industries get together to share ideas, information, and knowledge. Finding one of these in your area is the easiest route to take.

If you are unable to join a mastermind group, or if you want to focus on your business more directly, recruiting your own advisory board is the best option. An advisory board should give you objective advice, help you develop new strategic plans, assist in gauging future trends that might have an impact on your business, and help you see the big picture. Your advisory board members should view your business from different perspectives and challenge you with those views.

Advisory boards normally have no fiduciary responsibility. Some tend to be hands-on; others focus strictly on the big picture. Some meet monthly, others quarterly. An advisory board's approach and level of involvement depend on your needs and the board members' preferred role.

Business strategist Geri Stengel presents ten effective tips for creating an advisory board:

1. Determine the Objective of Your Advisory Board: Advisory boards can be general in scope or targeted to specific markets, industries, or issues such as adopting new technology or going global. They provide timely knowledge about trends and competitors, as well as identifying upcoming political, legislative, and regulatory developments. They can help you enter new businesses and look at your own operations with an open mind. Advisory boards can also be made up of customers and prospects who provide insights into product development and marketing issues.

2. Choose the Right People: Of course, when forming a board you need to understand its purpose, but you also need to know what specific skills to seek. In general, look for diverse skills, expertise, and experience. You want members to be problem solvers who are quick studies, have strong communications skills, and are open minded.

   Big names can be a bonus . . . but not always: Getting a heavyweight on your board of advisors can give you credibility, but it's also important to have members who are going to spend the time to give you thoughtful advice or are well connected and willing to make introductions.

3. Set Expectations: When inviting a prospective member to join your advisory board, you should lay down the ground rules about what is expected in terms of time, responsibilities, and term of office. Specify the areas in which you're seeking help. If the advisory board is going to discuss issues that include private information, members should be notified that they will be asked to sign a confidentiality agreement.

4. Compensate Your Advisory Board: Depending on whom you are asking and how involved you need them to be, compensation can vary from just providing food to covering expenses to stock options to cash payments to a combination of the four. Keep in mind that your members will likely benefit themselves in a variety of ways. Being on your board will expose them to ideas and perspectives they may have otherwise missed. It will also expand their own networks and provide them with a way of giving back.

5. Get the Most Out of Advisory Board Meetings: Prepare for meetings well in advance. Choose a site that is comfortable and free of distractions. Careful thought should be given to developing the agenda and managing the meeting. Solicit input for the agenda, and distribute important information ahead of time. Run the session as you would any professional meeting, and follow it with an action plan. The facilitator should know which experts to draw out and how to stimulate a dialogue. He or she should be results-oriented, as ideas without action aren't worth much. The minutes should be written up and circulated to top management. The notes should include recommendations on key issues.

6. Ask for Honesty: An advisory board must be open and frank, so don't be offended if you hear things you don't like. Your board will also suggest ways of correcting the problems they identify.

   If appropriate, encourage members to tell you about their mistakes so you can avoid making the same ones. You can learn a lot by finding out what other people did wrong.

7. Consider Alternative Feedback Methods: Getting the entire board together on a regular basis may not be possible. Instead, meet or have conference calls with specific members about topics relevant to their expertise as needed. E-mail is a great way to reach everyone and have them respond to you at their convenience.

8. Respect your Board's Contributions: Don't abuse or waste their time. Listen to what the board says. Sometimes, a business executive is so close to an issue, you can't see the forest for the trees. But remember: This isn't a corporate board, so you don't have to do everything they suggest. Ask yourself, "Does this work for my company? Am I comfortable with that?" Then make a decision.

9. Keep Board Members Informed: Once they're on the board, keep members excited about your business by giving them updates at times when you aren't soliciting their advice. The fact that they've agreed to be on your board means they care about your company, so keeping up-to-date will help them be of greater value to you. Remember that these people are evangelists for the company.

10. Fire Bad Board Members: If you realize you've made a bad choice, get rid of him or her. Unlike a board of directors, advisors can be replaced without a lot of legal headaches.[1]

There are usually at least a few people you know who can help you deal with certain issues or special problems that you may encounter in your business or profession. In lieu of specific knowledge, you must know in advance who to contact and where to go to get the information you need. Here are a few of our suggestions for the kinds of people you might wish to include on your advisory board:

People in your profession. As a rule, your best information sources will be people who are successfully doing what you want to do (perhaps in a different location or serving a different clientele). They will be aware of current trends and issues in your field and may have already faced some of the challenges you are now facing. Try to identify and speak with three to five individuals who fit this category. They will have current directories, manuals, and information about upcoming events related to your profession, as well as relationships with vendors that you may need to hire.

People who were in your profession. Find out why these people are no longer in the profession. What happened to their business? What are they doing now? Did they make the right decision to leave the profession? Talk with those who were successful and those who were not. Depending on the industry and the length of time the person has been away from it, this information may be valuable in helping you plan.

Authors. People who write or produce books, articles, audio-tapes, and videos on your profession are key subject experts. They usually have broad or deep knowledge about procedures, systems, technologies, tactics, and developments in your field. A few tips from these individuals could save you money and time.

Regulators. People who regulate, audit, or monitor professionals in your field can certainly tell you stories about the legal, procedural, and operational pitfalls that you might run into, and they probably know how to survive them. You may even discover legal loopholes that can make life and business easier.

Business consultants. Professionals use advisors and consultants to help them solve problems that they find difficult to handle alone, or to deal with impending change. Some consultants are generalists, others specialists. Most are skilled in assessing business problems and recommending solutions.

Members of professional organizations. People who are active members of trade, business, and professional organizations are prolific sources of information. Their membership gives them access to directories, newsletters, seminars, presentations, calendars of events, and more. By networking, they stay in touch with industry issues and trends. Spending time with them will help you discover new ways to do things.

Week 51 Action

Remember that your main goal is to seek information, advice, and expertise. Your task this week is to start planning your advisory board. Using Geri Stengel's suggestions, begin by outlining the purpose and objectives of your advisory board. What topics would you discuss? What advice would you seek? Who would you recruit to address those needs? How often would you meet? Where and how would you meet? What are your expectations for your advisory board members? Once you've answered these questions and thoroughly prepared this project, start asking specific people to serve on your advisory board. As you do this, you add a new level to your business. You instantly open yourself up to growth and opportunities. In addition, your network and the information you need to build your business will expand and grow.

☑ WEEK 52

Commit to Lifelong Learning

SINCE PRACTICALLY NO COLLEGE CURRICULUM in networking exists (despite its importance in the world of entrepreneurial business), you're pretty much left to your own devices to find training in the art and science of this set of skills. For the last time, we congratulate you on starting with this book, which you have now, perhaps, finished (unless you're the kind of person who reads the last page of a murder mystery first). But, as much as you've learned from this one book, we want to encourage you to continue your learning. In fact, we want you to commit to lifelong learning on the subject of networking.

Sounds like a huge assignment, doesn't it? Well, maybe it's not as daunting as it sounds. The truth is, networking is something you can train for on the job—in fact, that's the best way. By putting it into practice, you not only learn how to apply and fine-tune your approach, but you also build your business at the same time. In many ways, it's less work and more fun than some of the traditional approaches to building your business.

What's more, becoming a master networker is a journey, not a destination. You might reach the 29% by becoming a master networker, but that's not the end of your efforts, because a master networker is one who is constantly improving her skills and learning new ones. Now the challenge is to stay in the 29% and learn to secure your footing. Last week's strategy was to always think about what's next. There's no pot of gold at the end of the rainbow, just lots of gold along the way and more up ahead.

So, in your never-ending journey toward perfection, how do you improve on the basic networking plan that you've created through this book? We have several suggestions, in three categories, that will fit in with your activities as a businessperson and strengthen your network even as you learn.

First in your custom-tailored continuing education curriculum should be a commitment to keep reading. There are hundreds of articles and dozens of books out there on networking, word-of-mouth marketing, and referral marketing. We strongly recommend books like Bob Burg's *Endless Referrals*, Susan RoAne's *How to Work a Room* and *The Secrets of Savvy Networking*, Robyn Henderson's *Networking for $uccess*, Bill Cates's *Unlimited Referrals*, and Jan Vermeiren's *Let's Connect*. Other great books on these topics include *Truth or Delusion: Busting Networking's Biggest Myths*, *The World's Best Known Marketing Secret*, *Masters of Networking*, and *Business by Referral*. All of these will help you develop your own individual skills in this valuable process of business development.

Second: Practice! Practice! Practice! Apply the skills we talk about in this book. You can't learn to ride a bike just by reading a book; you have to get on and ride. The more you practice these ideas in organizations like BNI and chambers of commerce, the more you'll learn and feel comfortable with the process. Find groups that believe in education as part of their regular meetings. If they help by guiding you, you can practice these ideas as you participate.

Third, seek out reputable training programs on networking, more and more of which are being developed around the world to fill up the great void being ignored by colleges and universities. Two great programs we recommend are Brian Buffinni's referral training for the real estate industry, easily the best of its kind; and the Referral Institute, a company specializing in referral training programs for any business interested in creating a structured referral program as part of its business development efforts. Recently named as one of *Entrepreneur* magazine's Top 500 Franchises, the Referral Institute's focused approach is highly effective in training people to be skilled networkers while engaging in a structure referral marketing plan. Look also to your local business development and entrepreneur centers for workshops, experiential learning, and in-depth training in networking and word-of-mouth marketing.

Lifelong learning continually sharpens and hones your skills. Would you trust the growth of your enterprise to someone who's not skilled in one of the most effective ways to grow your business?

Week 52 Action

Your task this week is a twofer. First, review each week's strategy from this book and determine whether you need to improve your efforts in that area. Create a simple timetable to implement the ideas you haven't pursued.

Second, continue your learning on the subject of networking by enrolling in a course, attending a workshop, or reading the next book. Think about how the knowledge and skills you derive from these resources can continue to build and enhance your business by effective networking.

And here's one that is a task for every week. The next time you're at a networking meeting, look around the room and remember: It's not net-SIT; it's not net-EAT—it's netWORK!

Be one of the people in the room who truly knows how to work and leverage your network.

NOW WHAT?

OK, YOU'VE MADE IT TO THE END OF THIS BOOK. Now what? Our hope is that you have begun to network your business actively and vigorously—that you have ventured out of your cave! We hope you've seen the importance of creating networking goals for your business and have begun to focus on how you deliver your messages (especially to those in your network to whom you may not have been giving enough attention lately). We also hope that you have invested by becoming a giver to your network, and that ultimately, as you work your network effectively, you are beginning to see a much higher return on this networking investment.

This book is not meant to gather dust on your bookshelf. It is intended to become your personal word-of-mouth marketing plan, its strategies implemented week by week, for the growth of your business. Embed these strategies into the way you conduct your everyday business. Some, you will find, will carry on into your business plans for many years. Many are lifelong strategies that, with regular practice, will become a natural part of who you are and how you do business.

Remember, networking is not just something you do as a reaction when business is slow. The 29% Solution is simple . . . to fully integrate these strategies into the way you do business, making you a person with connections, respect, and a reliable stream of new business.

NOTES

Preface

1 Judith S. Kleinfeld, "Could It Be a Big World After All? The 'Six Degrees of Separation Myth,'" *Society*, 2002.

Introduction

1 See Ivan R. Misner and Don Morgan, *Masters of Success: Proven Techniques for Achieving Success in Business and Life* (Irvine: Entrepreneur Press, 2004).

Week 1 Strategy: Set Networking Goals

1 Deanna Tucci Schmitt is the owner of BNI Western Pennsylvania. She can be reached at 150 East Highland Avenue, McMurray, PA 15317, 724-941-0101, or at dtschmitt@bni.com.

2 Steven Covey, *The 7 Habits of Highly Effective People* (New York: Simon & Schuster, 1989).

Week 8 Strategy: Diversify Your Contacts

1 *Wayne Baker, Achieving Success Through Social Capital: Tapping the Hidden Resources in Your Personal and Business Networks* (San Francisco: Jossey-Bass, 2000), 85.

2 Ibid., 83.

Week 10 Strategy: Reconnect with People from the Past

1 Jill Green is the Director of Coaching for the Referral Institute UK. She can be reached at 11 Clayfield, Brimsham Park, Yate, South Gloucestershire, BS37 7PE, +44 870 050 17 15 or team@referralinstitute.co.uk.

Week 13 Strategy: Join a Web-Based Networking Group

1 David Teten and Scott Allen, T*he Virtual Handshake: Opening Doors and Closing Deals Online* (New York: AMACOM/American Management Association, 2005).

2 Michael Jones, "Leveraging Social Networking Sites to Generate Business," About: Entrepreneurs, http://entrepreneurs.about.com/od/onlinenetworking/a/socnetsites.htm.

3 AOL News and Broadcast Center, "AOL Acquires Userplane," August 14, 2006, http://press.aol.com/article_display.cfm?article_id=1031&section_id=14.

4 Ibid.

Week 14 Strategy: Become Magnetic

1 *Merriam-Webster's Collegiate Dictionary*, 11th ed., s.v. "Magnetic."

Week 21 Strategy: Be "ON" 24/7

1 Baker, *Achieving Success Through Social Capital*, 8.

2 Ibid., 9.

Week 23 Strategy: Have Purposeful Meal Meetings

1 Keith Ferrazzi with Tahl Raz, *Never Eat Alone: And Other Secrets to Success, One Relationship at a Time* (New York: Doubleday, 2005), 96.

2 Ibid., chap. 21, "Find Anchor Tenants and Feed Them."

3 Ibid., 192.

4 His Holiness the Dalai Lama, *Ethics for the New Millennium* (New York: Riverhead, 1999), 62.

Week 25 Strategy: Seek Out a Referral Networking Group

1 Julien Sharp, "Business Referral Study: Replication of 1993 BNI® Study" (Kennedy-Western University, Agora Hills, CA, 1006).

Week 29 Strategy: Ask Your Own Questions

1 Bob Burg, *Endless Referrals: Network Your Everyday Contacts into Sales* (New York: McGraw-Hill, 1998), 20.

Week 37 Strategy: Write Your Own Identity

1 See Ivan R. Misner and Don Morgan, *Masters of Success: Proven Techniques for Achieving Success in Business and Life* (Irvine: Entrepreneur Press, 2004) 4, 46–47, 236.

Week 46 Strategy: Ask for Referrals

1 Mark Sheer, *Referrals: Reap Rewards, Earn More Money in Less Time, and Have More Fun* (M. Sheer Seminars, 1993).

2 Ibid.

Week 49 Strategy: Become the Hub Firm of a Power Team

1 Ivan R. Misner, *The World's Best-Known Marketing Secret: Building Your Business with Word-of-Mouth Marketing*, Revised ed. (Austin: Bard Press, 1999).

Week 50 Strategy: Become a Networking Mentor

1 Peter F. Drucker, *Management: Tasks, Responsibilities, Practices*. (New York: HarperCollins, 1993), 463.

2 "Characteristics of a Good Mentor," www.sonic.net/~mfreeman/mentor/mentchar.htm.

Week 51 Strategy: Recruit an Advisory Board for Your Business

1 Geri Stengel, "Ten Tips to Creating an Effective Advisory Board," www.stengelsolutions.com/tips19.htm. Geri Stengel is the president of Stengel Solutions, a full-service "strategic planning and marketing firm specializing in solutions for industry leaders, growth businesses, and nonprofits" (www.stengelsolutions.com). Geri can be reached at 212-362-3088, by e-mail at geri@stengelsolutions.com, or through the Web site. Or you can write her at Stengel Solutions, 210 West 70th Street, 510, New York, NY 10023.

BIBLIOGRAPHY

Books

Baker, Wayne. *Achieving Success Through Social Capital: Tapping the Hidden Resources in Your Personal and Business Networks.* San Francisco: Jossey-Bass, 2000.

Cates, Bill. *Get More Referrals Now!* New York: McGraw-Hill, 2004.

Collins, Jim. *Good to Great: Why Some Companies Make the Leap . . . and Others Don't.* New York: Harper-Collins, 2001.

Covey, Steven. *The 7 Habits of Highly Effective People.* New York: Simon & Schuster, 1989.

Ferrazzi, Keith, with Tahl Raz. *Never Eat Alone.* New York: Doubleday, 2005.

Fisher, Donna, and Sandy Vilas. *Power Networking: 55 Secrets for Personal & Professional Success.* Austin: MountainHarbor Publications, 1992.

His Holiness the Dalai Lama. *Ethics for the New Millennium.* New York: Riverhead, 1999.

Misner, Ivan R. *Masters of Networking: Building Relationships for Your Pocketbook and Soul.* Austin: Bard Press, 2004.

Misner, Ivan R., and Robert Davis. *Business by Referral: A Sure-Fire Way to Generate New Business.* Austin: Bard Press, 1998.

Misner, Ivan R., and Don Morgan. *Masters of Success: Proven Techniques for Achieving Success in Business and Life.* Irvine: Entrepreneur Press, 2004.

Misner, Ivan R. *The World's Best-Known Marketing Secret: Building Your Business with Word-of-Mouth Marketing.* Revised Edition. Atlanta: Bard Press, 2002.

RoAne, Susan. *How to Work a Room: Your Essential Guide to Savvy Socializing.* Revised Edition. New York: Collins, 2000.

Schumacher, Linda H. *Ready Set Succeed: How Successful Projects Triumph over Business as Usual.* Carscallen Press, 2006.

Stielstra, Greg. *Pyro-Marketing: The Four-Step Strategy to Ignite Customer Evangelists and Keep Them for Life.* Collins, 2005.

Electronic Articles

Whatis.com

www.hillnews.com/thehill/export/TheHill/Features/CapitalLiving/071905_rules.htm

PRW at www.press-release-writing.com

Jones, Michael. "Leveraging Social Networking Sites to Generate Business," About: Entrepreneurs, http://entrepreneurs.about.com/od/onlinenetworking/a/socnetsites.htm.

Misner, Ivan. "Building a Think Tank for Your Business." Entrepreneur.com, October 27, 2003, http://www.entrepreneur.com/marketing/marketingideas/networkingcolumnistivanmisner/article65206.html.

———. "How Deep is Your Network?" Entrepreneur.com, February 24, 2006, http://www.entrepreneur.com/marketing/marketingideas/networkingcolumnistivanmisner/article83756.html.

———. "Why We Need to Teach Networking." Entrepreneur.com, September 27, 2004, http://www.entrepreneur.com/marketing/marketingideas/networkingcolumnistivanmisner/article72742.html.

ABOUT THE AUTHORS

IVAN R. MISNER, PHD, is the founder and chairman of BNI, the world's largest business networking organization. Founded in 1985, BNI now has thousands of chapters throughout every populated continent of the world. Each year, BNI generates millions of referrals, resulting in billions of dollars' worth of business for its members.

Dr. Misner's doctoral degree is from the University of Southern California. He has written nine books, including the *New York Times* bestseller *Masters of Networking* and his number-one bestseller *Masters of Success*. He is a monthly columnist for Entrepreneur.com and is chairman of the board of the Referral Institute, a referral-training company with trainers around the world. He has taught business and social capital courses at several universities and sits on the board of trustees for the University of the Rockies.

Called the "Father of Modern Networking" by CNN and the "Networking Guru" by *Entrepreneur* magazine, Dr. Misner is one of the world's leading experts on business networking and has been a keynote speaker for major corporations and associations throughout the world. He has been featured in the *Los Angeles Times, Wall*

Street Journal, and *New York Times*, as well as on numerous television and radio shows on networks such as CNN, CNBC, and the BBC in London.

Dr. Misner also serves on the board of directors for the Haynes Children Center. He is the founder of the BNI-Misner Charitable Foundation and was recently named "Humanitarian of the Year" by the *Daily Bulletin*. He lives with his wife, Elisabeth, and their three children in Claremont, California. In his spare time (!), he is also an amateur magician and a black belt in karate.

MICHELLE R. DONOVAN, M.ED. is known as "the Referability Expert" in Pittsburgh, Pennsylvania. She is the owner and founder of Pinnacle Training Services, offering customized business development seminars. In addition, she owns and operates the Referral Institute of Western Pennsylvania, specializing in referral marketing programs and referral coaching.

In addition, Michelle has been a guest faculty member at both the Office of Continuing Education at Penn State Beaver campus and the University of Pittsburgh's Katz Center for Executive Education.

Michelle is a contributing author to *Girls at the Center: Girls and Adults Learning Science Together* and has published multiple contributions to the *Training and Development Sourcebook*. She has published numerous articles on business networking and referral marketing in professional journals and publications and has presented at national and local conferences.

Michelle earned a bachelor's degree in education from Slippery Rock University and a master's degree in adult education from Widener University. She is a certified Instructor of Trainers for the Girl Scouts of the United States of America, a trained facilitator for the interpersonal skills training program Working PeopleSmart®, and a regional instructor for the Certified Networker program from the Referral Institute.

As a facilitator, Michelle combines energy and fun with meaningful substance through real-life application to learning. The key to her success is a supportive partner and surrounding herself with exceptional people. In her spare time, she makes homemade wine, rides her motorcycle, plays billiards, and really enjoys camping and fishing with family.

ACKNOWLEDGMENTS

I would like to express my deepest gratitude to the following people for providing me with support and strength throughout this process.

To Alyssa M. Krasinskas—my rock and foundation. Your confidence in me fuels my creativity and passion for life.

To James and Rose Donovan—the creators of my spirit. You provided the encouragement to always reach for my fullest potential.

To Deanna Tucci Schmitt—the linchpin behind this book. Your ongoing friendship, guidance, and support continues to lift me to higher levels.

To The Circle of Excellence—my BNI chapter. You are the inspiration behind this book. Your friendship and commitment to excellence inspires me on a weekly basis to be an exceptional networker.

And finally, to the many clients, colleagues, and friends who continue to see the value in business networking and referral marketing. My wish for you is that you not only get into the 29%, but that you also maintain the commitment to stay there!

I consider myself blessed to have you all in my life!

—Michelle R. Donovan

Above all, I would like to thank my family—Beth, Trey, Cassie, and Ashley—for their love and support. The four of you have always been a constant source of inspiration for me, and though I feel extremely privileged to be able to travel the world, you will always be the reasons I can't wait to get home.

I would also like to thank Julien Sharp and Jeff Morris for their outstanding talents in editing this manuscript. Both of you contributed greatly to the quality of this book and your hard work is very much appreciated.

Lastly, I must mention two groups of people that I am very grateful to—Greenleaf Book Group and the entire BNI team. Greenleaf Book Group has been a pleasure to work with throughout this entire publication process, and I cannot thank the BNI team enough for keeping everything running smoothly during all the times I've been away writing.

—Ivan R. Misner, PhD

INDEX

REFERRAL® INSTITUTE

THE REFERRAL INSTITUTE is a leading referral training organization with franchises, trainers, and coaches around the world. The organization teaches business professionals how to harness the power of referral marketing to drive sales for long-term, sustainable business growth by referral. Founded in 2001, the Referral Institute began developing training materials specific to referral marketing. Today, the Referral Institute is a franchised company. Senior partner Dr. Ivan Misner and president Mike Macedonio are proud to announce that Entrepreneur.com, having noticed how quickly the Referral Institute was growing, recognized it as one of the top 500 franchised companies in the world.

The Referral Institute's mission is to direct professionals to proactively increase their business through implementing structured referral strategies. In total, the Referral Institute provides the world's leading material on referral marketing in three different areas:

Referral Marketing Training. The Referral Institute offers students one-day programs as well as courses covering several modules over ten to twelve weeks. The Pipeline Program, our signature class, requires participants to attend the class with a referral source. The one-day Pipeline Seminar teaches a simple, highly manageable referral process by which participants leave the training having already scheduled appointments with qualified prospects.

Another popular program is our Understanding GEMS program. This one-day program teaches how your behavioral style affects your referability. Students participate in a behavioral assessment, are taught how to recognize behavioral styles and adapt to them, and learn how to work with and develop referral sources. Students realize that each behavioral style is truly a "gem" to work with, if you know how!

Our ten- to twelve-week course is called Certified Networker. This course is truly a foundation for understanding, developing, and tracking your referral business. In most cases, Certified Networker will simply change the way business owners do business. It narrows their target market, provides them with mission statements, and shows them how profitable it can be to develop referral sources by being strategic. Certified Networker is a must for anyone new to referral marketing,

Referral Marketing Coaching. As students of the Referral Institute begin learning the formulas and philosophies necessary to implement referral marketing, they are also encouraged to have accountability. Our coaches have received intense training on behavioral styles and referral marketing plans, and they are required to graduate from our Directive Coaching School. Being coached by a Referral Institute coach will ensure your success in creating the long-term referral sources that bring you more business by referral.

Referral Marketing Consulting. Our consultants will design and implement customized referral marketing plans with businesses and corporate clients. Combining training, coaching, and collaboration, our consultants are able to tailor the Referral Institute's programs to work with one employee or hundreds of employees around the world. This is the ultimate process for integrating referral marketing into your business or your corporate culture.

Please browse the Web site at www.referralinstitute.com to learn more about referral marketing as well as how to attend a Referral Institute training program in your area. You may contact the organization at info@referralinstitute.com to talk about growing your business by generating qualified referrals.

BNI®

BNI, THE WORLD'S LARGEST business networking organization, was founded by Dr. Ivan Misner in 1985 as a way for businesspeople to generate referrals in a structured, professional environment. The organization, now the world's largest referral business network, has thousands of chapters with tens of thousands of members on every populated continent. Since its inception, BNI members have passed millions of referrals, generating billions of dollars in business for the participants.

The primary purpose of the organization is to pass qualified business referrals to its members. The philosophy of BNI may be summed up in two simple words: Givers Gain. If you give business to people, you will get business from them. BNI allows only one person per profession to join a chapter. The program is designed to help businesspeople develop long-term relationships, thereby creating a basis for trust and, inevitably, referrals. The mission of BNI is to help members increase their business through a structured, positive, and professional word-of-mouth program that enables them to develop long-term, meaningful relationships with quality business professionals.

To visit a chapter near you, contact BNI via e-mail at bni@bni.com or visit its Web site at www.bni.com.

Ivan Misner's Networking Series of Books

- *The World's Best-Know Marketing Secret: Building Your Business with Word-of-Mouth Marketing*, $18.95, paperback

- *Masters of Networking: Building Relationships for Your Pocketbook and Soul*, $18.95, paperback

- *Masters of Success: Proven Techniques for Achieving Success in Business and Life*, $18.95, paperback

- *It's in the Cards!: Getting the Biggest Impact from Your Smallest Ad*, $20.00, hardcover

- *Truth or Delusion?: Busting Networking's Biggest Myth*, $19.95, hardcover

- *Business by Referral: A Sure-Fire Way to Generate New Business*, $18.95, paperback

For more information about these titles, visit www.bni.com or call toll free 1-800-688-9394 (1-909-608-7575 in Southern California) 24 hours a day, 7 days a week. Quantity discounts are available. VISA/MasterCard/American Express.

To order by mail, enclose check with your order payable to: BNI, 545 College Commerce Way, Upland, CA 91786.